This book to be returned on or before the last date below.

H & G

How to RESEARCH
YOUR HOUSE

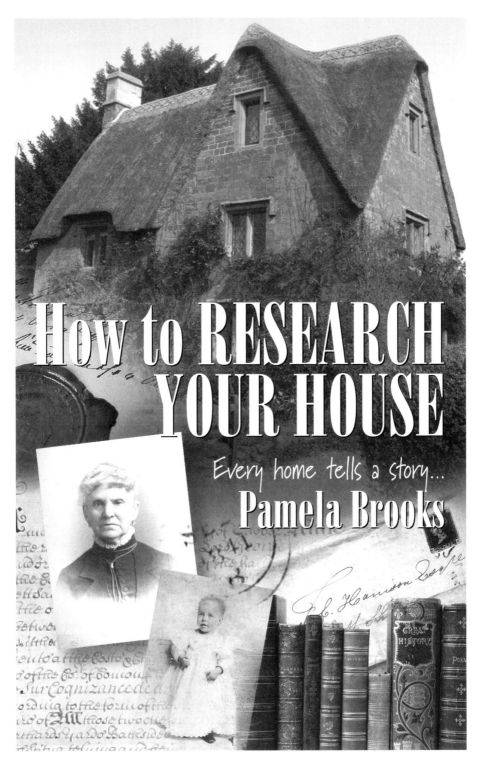

How to RESEARCH YOUR HOUSE

Every home tells a story...

Pamela Brooks

howtobooks

Published by How To Books Ltd
Spring Hill House
Spring Hill Road
Begbroke, Oxford OX5 1RX
Tel: (01865) 375794. Fax: (01865) 379162
email: info@howtobooks.co.uk
www.howtobooks.co.uk

British Library Cataloguing in Publication Data
A catalogue record for this book is available from the British
Library

ISBN 13: 978 1 84528 165 6

Cover design by Baseline Arts Ltd, Oxford
Produced for How to Books by Deer Park Productions, Tavistock
Typeset by Pantek Arts Ltd, Maidstone, Kent
Printed and bound by Cromwell Press Ltd, Trowbridge, Wiltshire

NOTE: The material contained in this book is set out in good
faith for general guidance and no liability can be accepted
for loss or expense incurred as a result of relying in particular
circumstances on statements made in this book. Laws and
regulations are complex and liable to change, and readers should
check the current position with the relevant authorities before
making personal arrangements.

Contents

List of Illustrations

Acknowledgements

I owe thanks to several people for help during the writing of this book. These include: Wendy Sterry and the staff of the Norfolk Heritage Centre in the Millennium Library, Norwich, for help in locating documents and maps; Freda Wilkins-Jones and the staff of the Norfolk Record Office in Norwich for help in locating documents and their kind permission to use photographs of maps; the Ordnance Survey, for their kind permission to use photographs of maps; Donna Kissinger, for her kind permission to use a photograph of Mill House; Ron and Gay Sewell, for the loan of documentation and their patience when I was asking interminable questions about the house; Nikki Read and Dorothy Lumley, for giving me the chance to do the research I'd wanted to do since I was very small and overheard an interesting conversation between my parents about the ghost of our house. And last, but very far from least: Gerard Brooks, for putting up with copies of ancient maps all over the house and doing the school run on my 'record office days' to give me extra time in the archives; and Christopher and Chloë Brooks, for their patience in letting their mother take them on field trips to research architectural features and windmills.

For my parents, Ron and Gay Sewell, with love

1

Introduction

This chapter discusses the different strands to researching the history of your house:

- the building itself
- what it was used for
- who lived there
- and any events that happened there.

RESEARCHING THE HISTORY OF YOUR HOUSE

Finding out about the history of your house can be absolutely fascinating. Even if your house is modern the site may be part of a former large estate, or there may have been an earlier building on the same site as yours. That's still part of the history of your house.

Putting together a jigsaw puzzle

Finding out about when the house was built, who lived there, what the building was used for and anything that happened there is like putting together a jigsaw puzzle. It's very unlikely that all the information you need for your research will be together in one place, and you'll need to work with several different types of sources to tease out the information. You may find that the trail will grow cold in one strand of research, and then suddenly a lead will turn up in a different area which links back to the original strand.

You might not be able to trace the history of your house right back to the very beginning, because some of the evidence (such as the earliest title deeds or manorial records) may not have survived; and you may find that even if you have a fairly good trail there are mysterious holes that you might never be able to fill.

You might also have to take another look at sources you've already used, if you discover information elsewhere that sheds new light on those sources. Some sources may give you information on different aspects of your research; others will help you confirm evidence from different sources. For example:

- Title deeds can tell you about who owned the building as well as when the building changed hands and any special covenants (such as building restrictions). If the deeds go back far enough they may tell you when the house was built.
- Maps can help you pinpoint when the house was built. It's also very useful to compare different types of maps, as well as maps from different dates, to help you see if the building was extended (or if outbuildings were knocked down). Tithe and enclosure maps usually come with extra written evidence (the 'award' or 'apportionment'), which may tell you who owned or occupied the building and also the land or buildings on the boundaries of the property. They may also tell you if the land belonged to a manor at one point, in which case you'll be able to check through the manorial records for more evidence.
- Trade directories (particularly ones towards the end of the nineteenth century) can help you find out if your house was used as a shop, pub, beerhouse, factory or chapel during a certain time period, and may also tell you who lived or worked there.
- Census returns can show who lived in the property and their occupations. You may be able to confirm the details and even learn extra information by cross-referencing the information you find in the census returns with that from the trade directories.

TYPES OF SOURCES

The types of information you'll use fall into four categories:

- **Primary** – usually written (though sometimes printed) original records, such as title deeds, manorial rolls, assize records, wills, census returns, taxations lists and electoral rolls.
- **Secondary** – may be transcriptions of records, monographs on a village written by an antiquarian, standard local histories, contemporary or retrospective articles on people or places or trades, websites, or architectural surveys such as Pevsner's *Building of England* series.
- **Oral** – recollections of neighbours or other people who've lived in the local area for a long time.
- **Physical** – the place itself, old photographs or drawings, aerial photographs, architectural plans and maps.

Although you won't necessarily need an in-depth knowledge of Latin and palaeography (old handwriting) for documents after about 1750, researching the history of your house means that you will be dealing with a real variety of documents, including title deeds (or abstracts of title), census returns, wills, maps and apportionments, tax assessments and poll books.

You'll be able to do some of the research from the physical structure of the building, but to do other parts you will need to visit local libraries and record offices, or even the National Archives at Kew. You'll also need to consult registers (such as the electoral roll), trade directories and possibly back issues of local newspapers.

In the record office and library archives you may be able to see the originals of some documents. For documents that are heavily used (such as census returns, parish registers and old copies of newspapers), or ones which are 'unfit for production' (i.e. very fragile or damaged), you are more likely to use versions on 'microform' – that is, microfiche or microfilm. These need special readers, which magnify the documents so they're easier to read; though do bear in mind that even so the type size of early nineteenth-century newspapers is tiny, and some of the documents (particularly the handwritten ones) are filmed in negative (i.e. white writing on a black background). Together with the fact that early handwriting can be a bit indistinct and the ink on the documents is sometimes faded, this means that microfiche and microfilm records can be very wearing to read for long periods.

WORKING BACKWARDS

The important thing is to start with what you know and work backwards through the primary sources. This is because:

- The further back you go, the harder handwriting is to read; you may also find that abbreviations are more difficult to work out. As the format of legal documents tends to be the same down the years, you'll be in a better position to work out difficult words and abbreviations in earlier documents if you're already familiar with the same phrases used in later documents.
- Particularly with census returns, the further back you go the less likely it is that the property will have a street number or house name. It's easier to trace back through the records from occupant details that you know as definite, and take into account records of neighbouring properties to help you pinpoint yours.

USING THIS BOOK

The following chapters will guide you through the kind of records you'll need, where to find them and how to use them, as well as tips for dating the property architecturally. Throughout I'll be using examples from my own research on the history of the cottage where I grew up, in the Norfolk market town of Attleborough. I thought I knew most of the facts before I started researching, but there were a few surprises in store for me.

The appendices show how I traced through different sources of information to create a record of who owned the property and who lived there. There's also a copy of a transcribed title abstract, a list of common abbreviations in title deeds, and lists of useful reference books and websites.

(2)

Preparing to Research

This chapter deals with:

◆ the work you'll need to do before you start looking at primary sources.

RECORDING THE PROPERTY AS IT IS NOW

Making a record of how the property is now will help you compare the present-day building against earlier photographs, plans or sketches. You may see some changes in the structure of the buildings, or changes in the neighbouring buildings. Useful tools are as follows:

Photographs
◆ An overall photograph of the building – do this from several angles and try to include features of neighbouring buildings on some of them.
◆ Close-ups of original features such as windows, chimneys, rooflines, doors, date marks, fire plaques, etc.

Plan of the property
Make a rough sketch as well as one that's to scale, and make several photocopies so you can use them to make comparisons with other plans (see Chapters 6 and 7). Include:

◆ The boundaries of the land; it's also useful to make notes of the position of neighbouring properties, so that you can compare them with earlier plans or maps.
◆ The position, shape and size of the building, including any outbuildings.
◆ The position, shape and size of any windows or doors.

Internal measurements are also useful as they will help you work out the thickness of the walls – as a rule of thumb, older walls tend to be thicker than more modern walls.

Sketch of the property's elevations

Make a sketch of the front, sides and back, including measurements.

WHERE IS THE PROPERTY SITUATED?

It sounds an obvious question, but boundaries of parishes and administrative districts tend to change over the years. Make a note of the name of:

- the parish;
- the Hundred (the old administrative unit);
- the ecclesiastical district (deanery);
- the electoral district;
- the council district;
- the poor law district (or union);
- the manor or estate owner.

In the example of our case study, Mill House is situated in the parish of Attleborough, which was in the Shropham Hundred of Norfolk. Together with the Guiltcross Hundred, the Shropham Hundred was in the Deanery of Rockland. Attleborough was also part of the Wayland Union under the poor law. In the present day Attleborough is in the administrative district of Breckland Council, and is in the electoral district of South West Norfolk.

CHANGES TO THE PROPERTY

Do you know if the house's name or number has changed? What about the street name? Do you know if the house itself has been extended, rebuilt or refaced? If you know of any definite changes make a list of them, including dates.

Mill House is just off the junction between present-day Connaught Plain and the High Street. As far as I knew, the High Street (which was the main street through the town) had always been called that. However, I discovered (via the census records) that the street had previously been known as Levell Street and Mere (or Meer) Street. According to an advertisement in the local newspaper the street was known as Town Street in about 1804; it was also known as 'the turnpike road' in the eighteenth century.

WHAT DO YOU ALREADY KNOW?
Sources
Look at the sources you already have. For example:

- **Title deeds** – these should tell you the names and occupations of previous owners, when the property changed hands, and any covenants attached to the property (for example, building lines beyond which any owner shouldn't extend the property, or any conditions such as not keeping certain types of livestock on the land). The deeds may go back far enough to tell you when the property was built. If there is an enfranchisement deed as part of the bundle, this means the land and/or building once belonged to a manor, so you may also find records of the property and its occupants in the manorial rolls.
- **Sales particulars** (whether very recent or very old) – these may give a detailed description of the property, which you can compare with the building as it is now. For example, the sales particulars may refer to outbuildings that have long since been pulled down.
- **Maps or plans** – you can use these for comparison with your present-day records.
- **Photographs or sketches** – you can use these for comparison with your present-day records.

For example, for Mill House my parents had a copy of the abstract of title going back to 1850; there were also sales particulars from 1912, which included a plan of the area and showed who owned neighbouring plots of land and buildings. From those two sets of information I could work out who owned or occupied the building from 1850 until we moved in. Sadly, there were no photographs of the house or garden available from any earlier date than when my family moved in. There were however references to the mill itself on various maps dating back to 1797, and I knew there would be reference to the land on the tithe map dating from the early to mid-nineteenth century and the enclosure map dating from 1812–15.

I discovered a sale notice in the newspaper archive, which actually told me when the house was built. Because the property included a mill at one point, I knew there was a good chance the property would be listed in the nineteenth-century trade directories, and it was also possible that the land had been part of a manor as it was in the centre of the town – so there were plenty of leads to follow up at the record office and local heritage centre.

Date the property was built

Do you know exactly – or even approximately – when the property was built? You may be able to narrow it down by using maps. See Chapter 6 for more details about the different types of maps that can help with your research.

Before I started my research into the history of the house, I knew from the deeds that Mill House existed in 1850; obviously there was a mill nearby at some point, which gave the house its name. The mill was marked by a little 'windmill' symbol (of an x-shaped cross on an oval, sitting on top of a triangular post) on Faden's Map of Norfolk in 1797 (see picture 6.9 on page 96) and there was a similar symbol on Bryant's Map of Norfolk in 1826, which had a slightly larger scale. However, neither of these two maps was detailed enough to show the cottage itself. So all I knew definitely was that the cottage existed in 1850 (and, from the architectural evidence, probably before then) and the mill was there from at least 1797.

Listed buildings

Is the building listed? If it's over 150 years old it may be recorded on the Department of the Environment's list of buildings they think are worthy of preservation. English Heritage holds descriptions and some photographs of listed buildings on their website, www.english-heritage.org.uk – a particularly good database on the site is Images of England www.imagesof england.org.uk/, which holds photographic records of listed buildings. However, note that the description of the property is unlikely to be very detailed as it's based on a very brief external inspection.

There is also a list prepared for the Royal Commission on Historical Monuments, which is rather more detailed and sometimes includes maps and plans.

I checked the lists for properties in Attleborough. I wasn't expecting to see Mill House on the Historical Monuments list, but I was disappointed to discover that it wasn't on the Department of the Environment's List. There were also no records whatsoever of the mill.

Secondary sources

Is the building named in any secondary sources? (See Chapter 3 for more details about secondary sources.) These include:

◆ Pevsner's *Buildings of England* series.
◆ The *Victoria History of the Counties of England* series (*VCH* for short).
◆ Street/trade directories (if the building is not noted in the actual street lists, it may be mentioned in the potted history of the city, town or village).

I checked the secondary sources for Mill House. There was no mention of the building in Pevsner or in the *VCH*. However, the street directories were much more useful. *Pigot and Co's National Commercial Directory of Norfolk and Suffolk* for 1830 gave an intriguing reference to John Mann at 'Attleburgh Great Mill' as well as listing a mill owned by Thomas Dodd (near an area known in modern times as Dodd's Road, to the south of the town), one owned by William Harris at Rivett Lane (now known as Hargham Road), and ones owned by Robert Lovett and Robert Palmer at 'Bisthorpe' (now known as Besthorpe). Earlier directories named some millers, but not their exact locations within the town – which meant checking the census returns to see if I could fit names to locations.

Former use

Do you know if the building was formerly something other than a house? Examples are:

- a shop;
- a mill;
- a farm;
- a hospital;
- a workhouse;
- a school;
- a pub;
- a toll house.

For any of these there may be additional records you can look up, such as licensing registers for a pub, log books for a school, or minutes of the Board of Trustees for a hospital, workhouse, or school, or Turnpike Trust for a toll house.

There may also be contemporary articles in local newspapers about the building, for example when it was built or when the school, hospital or workhouse opened or closed, as well as who built or owned it, and who worked there. Local newspapers might also cover events at the building – if there was a flood or fire, for example, or if there was an epidemic at a school or workhouse, or if there was a royal visit or a visit by a celebrity to a school or hospital. (See Chapter 10 for more information about researching in newspapers.)

If the house involved a business such as a pub, shop or factory, there may also be advertisements in local newspapers or in the early twenti-eth-century trade directories.

Local historians may also have built databases or websites about partic-ular types of buildings such as mills or pubs; these may contain information about your building. There may also be organisations that specialise in the history of particular types of buildings, and who may be able to give you more information about your home.

For Mill House I knew that there had been a mill near to the house (because of the name of the cottage and also from the position of the mill marked on early maps of the county – Faden's Map of 1797 and Bryant's Map of 1826). So that meant that I could check trade directory listings for millers – and that in turn would help me cross-check against census records for occupants of the cottage, assuming that the miller lived near to his workplace.

WHICH SOURCES DO YOU NEED TO CONSULT?

Before you start to research, list what you need to look up and where to find it. These will be basically as follows:

Primary sources about the building

Deeds

The most recent deeds may be with your solicitor or held by your mortgage provider. Earlier deeds may have been given to the local record office by a former occupant, or they may have been lost, in which case you'll need to work back through other sources to try to dig up the information.

Land Registry

You can obtain a copy of the title register details and title plan for your property (in England and Wales) from the Land Registry via their online service at www.landregisteronline.gov.uk, for a small fee. The title plan is a plan of the property and shows boundaries. The register information usually includes:

- a description of the property;
- who owns it;
- the mortgage lender (if any);
- the price (if registered since 1 April 2000);
- rights of way (excluding public rights of way) or other rights affecting the property;
- restrictions or conditions.

If you don't have access to the internet you can get the information by post. Your nearest District Land Registry office or legal stationer will have the form you need to apply for a copy of the register.

The Land Registry may be able to supply you with information about previous transfers of the property (i.e. when it was bought or sold), but the searches through their records may take some time and be quite expensive. It's worth noting that the information in their files dates only from the time that the property was first registered with the Land Registry, which might be much later than the date when the property was built.

Manorial records

If the land was part of a manor at one point it may be listed in the rentals, extants or estate maps (see Chapter 8 for more details about manorial records). Your local record office may be able to help you find out where the documents are held.

Ordnance Survey Maps

Most libraries and record office have copies of the 1-inch series maps. There are excellent collections at the National Archives and the British Library. You can see the 6-inch editions online on the Old Maps website www.old-maps.co.uk. There may also be some earlier maps online, depending on your county's archive; for example, Norfolk has various maps (including aerial photography) at www.historic-maps.norfolk. gov.uk/ and East Sussex has pre-1813 maps at www.envf.port.ac.uk/geo/ research/historical/webmap/sussexmap/sussex.html.

Sales particulars

These may be in local record office collections of catalogues from sale houses/auctions, but you will need to know the precise date of the sale, to save having to wade through enormous amounts of information.

Building control plans and planning applications

These are held at local record offices, and at local building control or planning departments.

Road order maps and deposited plans

These are held at local record offices.

Glebe terriers

If the building belonged to the church these are held at your local record office or diocesan office.

Secondary sources about the building

Pevsner

The volumes of Pevsner's *Buildings of England* series covering your area are likely to be available at your local reference library as well as local bookshops.

The Victoria History of the Counties of England series
The volumes covering your area will be available at your local reference library. You may also be able to access some of the pages (particularly those referring to ecclesiastic buildings) at the British History Online website www.british-history.ac.uk.

Department of Environment list
This is available at your local council planning department, county council offices and most local reference libraries. It is also available at the National Monuments Record, Kemble Drive, Swindon SN2 2GZ. Photographs of buildings that were on the list in 2001 are available online at the English Heritage website Images of England: www.image-sofengland.org.uk/.

Standard local history
The history for your county should be available at your local reference library (for example, for Norfolk it's Blomefield's *An Essay Towards a Topographical History of the County of Norfolk*, in 11 volumes).

Monographs
Any monographs that may be relevant to your research (e.g. a book or pamphlet on the history of a particular building, parish, town or family) should be available at your local reference library.

Primary sources about the occupant

Deeds
Sources as above.

Land registry
Sources as above.

Census returns

The originals are kept at the Family Records Centre in London (part of the National Archives), but the ones for your county should also be available in your local record office and/or local studies centre on microfilm or microfiche. You can also search digital images and transcriptions of the 1901 census online at www.1901censusonline.com. It's free to search the indexes, although you'll need to pay a small fee to see the census pages and transcripts. You can also search the 1891 census at www.ancestry.co.uk. The Society of Genealogists also holds copies of the returns for 1841–61 and 1891 on microfilm.

Hearth tax assessments

Assessments for Michaelmas 1662 to Lady Day 1666 and for Michaelmas 1669 to Lady Day 1674 are in the National Archives, series E179. Other years are held in local record offices, either on microfilm or microfiche. Between 1666 and 1669 the tax was collected by commissions (freelance collectors, known as 'farmers') and few lists of taxpayers survive.

Land tax assessments

These are available at county record offices, on microfilm or microfiche. They are usually found in the quarter sessions, in the records of the Clerk of the Peace. For the 1798 assessments see the National Archives, series IR23 and IR24.

Poll tax assessments

These are kept at the National Archives in series E179 and E182, though your local record office may have some lists.

Window tax assessments

These are kept at county record offices.

Wills and administration grants

Your local record office may have copies of proved wills and administration grants on microfiche. There may also be probate inventories.

Primary sources about both building and occupant

Tithe maps and schedules

The National Archives hold copies of each map in series IR30 and each schedule in series IR29. Copies are also held at county record offices, usually on microfilm or microfiche as well, and diocesan record offices. You may also be able to access them online, depending on your library service.

Valuation Maps 1910–15

These are also known as the Domesday maps. The working plans are held at county record offices, though it's worth noting that not all record offices have complete collections of the maps. The record sheet plans are held at the National Archives. They're split by region, and within each region there are up to 22 districts. The references for the regions are as follows:

- London – IR121;
- South East – IR124;
- Wessex – IR125;
- Central – IR126;
- Anglia – IR127;
- Western – IR128;
- West Midland – IR129;
- East Midland – IR130;
- Welsh – IR131;
- Liverpool – IR132;
- Manchester – IR133;
- Yorkshire – IR134;
- Northern – IR135.

Enclosure award maps and hereditaments

These are held at your local record office and also at the National Archives in series MAF1.

Rate books

These are held at your local record office, though note that there may not be a complete series of rate books. It's more likely that there will be gaps.

Secondary sources about both building and occupant

Street/trade directories

These are held at local reference libraries and/or local record offices. There are also some searchable copies online at the University of Leicester Historical Directories website www.historicaldirectories.org. You may be able to buy facsimile copies in book or CD form; originals do turn up in antiquarian and second-hand bookshops, but tend to be expensive.

Local newspapers

Copies are held (usually on microfiche) in local reference libraries, often in the county's local studies area. Your local newspaper group may also have a library you can search through, though you'll probably need to book a time slot and pay a fee to use the library as well as further fees for any copies of material you want to take away. However, the good news is that they'll be able to advise about copyright if you want to publish any of their material.

Oral sources about both building and occupant

These might include:

◆ former occupants;
◆ neighbours;
◆ local historians.

RECORD-KEEPING

Organising your notes properly right from the start will save you a lot of time. If you just write everything down in a bound notebook, you won't risk losing anything – but you'll also have to spend ages finding it again! So you need to think about the information you're collecting, how you want to use it and the best way of retrieving the information quickly.

While I was researching the history of Mill House I tended to make notes in the library or record office by longhand in a notebook, then transferred my notes straight to the computer when I returned home. Although this method does carry a small risk of mistranscribing the data, when you're working in the small space next to a microfilm or microfiche reader it's an awful lot easier to write in a shorthand notebook than it is to balance a laptop computer on the edge of a desk or on your lap!

When typing up the data I tended to use tables, which allowed me to mimic the columns of rate books, census returns and the like. This also made it easier to transfer details to a list of known occupiers and/or owners.

Noting your sources

It's important to make a note of your sources because:

◆ You may need to refer to the source again later and if you've noted it properly it will save you time locating the information again.
◆ If you're publishing your research as an article or book, you need to list your sources either as footnotes or in a bibliography.

It's also worth making a note of sources you decide *not* to use (and why). You can easily forget over a period of time if you decided not to use a source, then waste time locating it again only to find that it's not useful.

The usual way of listing sources is:

- **Books** – A.N. Author, *Title of Book* (publication date), place of publication, publisher, page number.
- **Articles** – A.N. Author, 'Title of Article', *Title of Magazine*, volume number, issue number, (publication date), pages where the article appears.
- **Reports** – A.N. author, *Title of Report* (publication date), name of organisation issuing the report, report number.
- **Internet articles** – A.N. Author (date), 'Title of Article', *Title of Online Magazine [Online]*, volume number, issue number, available from [URL reference, i.e. in the form website.co.uk/pagename.html (date accessed).
- **Other internet documents** – A.N. Author (date, if given), *Title of Document [Online]*, available from [URL reference, i.e. in the form website.co.uk/pagename.html, (date accessed).

Your local record office will be able to give you information about how to record the sources for original documents – for example, the tithe map and apportionment for Attleborough in Norfolk would be recorded as NRO (standing for Norfolk Record Office) DN/TA 84 (which stands for Diocese of Norwich/Tithe Apportionment). Most record offices have a system of letters and numbers which they use to locate documents; the letters will give you an idea of what sort of document it is.

VISITING THE RECORD OFFICE

Before you visit the local history section of the library or the local record office it's worth doing some groundwork. Most country libraries and record offices have websites that contain answers to most of the questions you would ask. These include:

- How to get there (including parking and public transport).
- Whether you need a reader ticket and which documents you need to take with you to register for a ticket.
- Opening hours.
- Access for special needs.
- An online catalogue; this is useful for helping you find the basics, though the archivists will probably be able to give you more detailed advice when you get there. You can also see online catalogues at the Access to Archives (A2A) website www.a2a.org.uk
- Whether you need to book a seat, map table or microfilm/fiche reader in advance and how long the slot is.
- Whether you can use a digital camera or tape recorder; also whether you need a photography permit and how to obtain one.
- Information leaflets (these can help save time in locating references).
- Document production – how many you can order at once and how frequently they're fetched.

There are certain rules common to all archives, which basically are there to protect the documents and the rights of other users:

- No smoking.
- No eating or drinking, including sweets or gum.
- Use pencils only as ink, ballpoint, highlighter and gel pens are not erasable and can damage documents – so can the debris from pencil sharpeners and erasers, so if you need to sharpen your pencil you'll need to do it outside the search room.
- Leave all bags, coats, umbrellas, folders, laptop cases, plastic bags and briefcases in lockers.
- Switch off all mobile phones or put them on silent operation and don't use them in the area.
- Silence in the room so you don't disturb other researchers.

Things you will be allowed to take into the search rooms include:

◆ Laptop computers (but not the case – this also applies to cameras).
◆ Notebooks and loose papers.
◆ Pencils.
◆ Glasses.
◆ Money (e.g. for photocopying fees).

Some record offices give you a transparent plastic bag to hold your personal items while you're in the search room.

WORKING WITH ORIGINAL DOCUMENTS

If you haven't worked with original documents before, ask the librarian or archivist for help – it's part of their job to help new researchers. They'll show you how to use cushions to support the spines of books, and how to use the weights for rolled documents. A few rules of thumb, some of which are obviously common sense, but are still worth noting:

◆ Make sure your hands are clean and dry.
◆ Handle the documents as little as possible (the grease from your hands can cause damage) and try not to touch written text.
◆ Don't use a pencil to point out or follow entries, or put any other mark on the documents – use a piece of white acid-free paper instead under the line of text to help you keep your place. The record office will have these on request.
◆ Use pencils only for making notes, and don't use a rubber or sharpener in the search room.
◆ Put bound volumes on stands, wedges or cushions to support their spines, not flat on the table and turn the pages carefully.
◆ Make sure the whole document is on the table and nothing hangs over the edge otherwise it's easy to damage documents.

- Don't rest anything, including your hand, notebooks, papers or magnifying glasses, on the documents – if your document is in a roll or outsize, the record office staff will give you special weights to use.
- If you request a bundle of documents such as deeds, make sure you return them in the same order as you found them and don't mix them up with other document bundles.
- Take the documents back as soon as you've finished with them.
- Make a note of the references you used before you start making notes. If your search wasn't successful, make a note of what you looked for and that you failed to find it – it will save you going over the same ground in a few months' time when you've forgotten that you looked at this particular document or bundle.
- Return documents promptly and in the order you received them.
- For microfilm, when you've finished using the film wind it back onto the spool it was on originally.
- For both microfilm and microfiche, return it to the correct storage slot. You should also have a 'marker' (usually a coloured plastic box for a film or a card for fiches) to put in place of the microfilm or fiche you're using, with a label to show which machine is using it, to let other researchers or library staff know.
- Check with record office staff if you wish to trace something. If possible, place a clear plastic sheet between the tracing paper and the document to save wear and tear on the document.

Making copies

There are some restrictions on copying documents in a record office. Some documents can't be copied because:

- Copying will break the law of copyright (particularly with maps and illustrations).
- Copying could damage the binding of a book.
- The document is too fragile or delicate to be copied.

It's often possible to have printouts from microfilm or microfiche (for a fee), and you may be able to arrange photographic copies of more delicate material (again, for a fee). Flash photography isn't usually allowed and neither is the use of hand-held scanners.

Transcribing

When transcribing (making a handwritten or typed copy) from an original document, only write what's there – don't modernise the spelling. Spelling wasn't standardised until the eighteenth century, and you may also find names transcribed wrongly, misheard and even spelled according to dialect. If you write out an abbreviated word in full, put square brackets round the letters you've added so you have a clear record of what's there in the original and what you've added. If you're not sure what something says, either put a question mark before your interpretation of the word or leave a blank space between square brackets. For an example see Appendix 2, Transcription of Abstract of Title.

There are common abbreviations – C. T. Martin's *The Record Interpreter* is a superbly helpful resource here, as it gives Latin and French abbreviations, explains the conventions of abbreviations, gives a glossary of Latin words, and gives Latin versions of place names, first names and surnames. Denis Stuart's *Manorial Records* is also an excellent source of common Latin terms and you may find it useful to work through the examples for transcription/translation.

Appendix 1 contains a list of common English abbreviations in title deeds.

A couple of places to get you started on deciphering old handwriting are the course at the National Archives website www.nationalarchives. gov.uk/palaeography/ and the online palaeography tutorial from Cambridge University www.english.cam.ac.uk/ceres/ehoc/. There are also helpful books on reading old handwriting; the ones I found useful are listed in Appendix 5.

Copyright

The laws of copyright apply to transcriptions as well as to original material. If in doubt, ask the record office staff for advice. There is no copyright in fact (for example, that John Smith was born on 1 March 1800); but if someone has already transcribed parish records they own the copyright of the form in which the material is presented, so you would need to obtain permission before publishing it.

Secondary Sources

This chapter looks at:

♦ the secondary sources of information about a building.

PEVSNER

The *Buildings of England* series by Nikolaus Pevsner is the classic architectural guide to buildings in each county. There is a rolling programme of updates – the information does change between editions, so it's worth checking the previous edition as well as the latest one. The building you're looking at may be listed in some detail if it's architecturally significant.

There's a descriptive gazetteer arranged alphabetically by town/village name. For a major city the buildings are listed within street order and the significant buildings are listed along with:

♦ A note of when it was built.
♦ A description of the building.
♦ Points of interest, such as which architect worked on restoration or alterations.
♦ A brief historical note (for example, the North-West and South Norfolk edition refers to Nos 1–2 Prospect Terrace in Attleborough; it mentions that the clasped purlin roof was one of the last built in Norfolk).

For towns and villages only the significant buildings are listed. Only the larger towns have 'perambulations' (i.e. a street-by-street look at the architecture); smaller villages may have references only to a church and one or two buildings that Pevsner and his associates considered worthy of note.

In the case of Mill House in Attleborough, the Pevsner volume on Norfolk containing the town (Norfolk North-West and South) doesn't mention the building at all.

VICTORIA COUNTY HISTORY

The *Victoria History of the Counties of England* (*VCH* for short) covers most counties. The series was originally started in 1899 and was dedicated to Queen Victoria, hence the name. The volumes are usually found in the 'outsize volume' section of the reference library and have a red cover. The most important section for looking at the history of a building is the topographical section, which deals with the cities, towns and villages within the county in turn and looks at buildings such as almshouses, manor houses and other important buildings. Some of the *VCH* are available online at British History Online www.british-history.ac.uk/.

In the case of Mill House in Attleborough, the *VCH* doesn't mention the building at all.

DEPARTMENT OF ENVIRONMENT LIST

Department of Environment lists (i.e. 'listed buildings') are published for each local authority area and contain short historical and architectural descriptions of the buildings of historical interest. These lists should be available at your local council planning department, county council offices and most local reference libraries, as well as at the National Monuments Record in Swindon. There are three categories in the list:

- **Grade I** – buildings of national importance or of exceptional interest.
- **Grade II*** – particularly important buildings of more than special interest.
- **Grade II** – buildings of special interest that need preservation – roughly 93% of listed buildings fall into this category.

Mill House in Attleborough is not listed as a building of historical interest, despite its age.

STANDARD LOCAL HISTORY

Your local library should be able to advise you where to see a copy of the standard local history for your county. This may contain references to your building, but it depends on how much detail the history contains – you may find that your village, for example, isn't even mentioned.

The standard local history for Norfolk is the 11-volume work of Francis Blomefield. However, the volume covering the history of Attleborough doesn't mention Mill House or the mill.

MONOGRAPHS

Eighteenth- and nineteenth-century gentlemen often wrote monographs – scholarly research on one particular subject, such as a building or a family or bridges within a town. It's worth checking with your local library to see if there's a parish history or monograph which might cover the geographical area around your house. Or there may be a short biography of someone who once lived in your property.

WEBSITES

Local historians often set up websites with a wealth of detail about buildings and people. Family historians may already have transcribed some of the census records from your area, or lists of people within a certain occupatuion. A good starting place for these is Genuki www.genuki.org.uk/; though do note that the material is usually copy-right, so if you're planning to publish your research you'll need to get permission to use their information.

There may also be websites with old photographs of the area you're researching. For example, in the Norwich area there's a superb website dedicated to the photography of George Plunkett, covering the city from 1930 onwards www.the-plunketts.freeserve.co.uk/; sadly, there isn't one covering Attleborough. I was delighted to discover that there was a web-site devoted to the mills of Norfolk www.norfolkmills.co.uk/, which included photographs – but of the mills I knew about in the Attleborough area, four in Attleborough itself and two in Besthorpe, only the two Besthorpe ones had an entry, there were no photographs of the four Attleborough mills. There was, however, a reference to 'Attleburgh Great Mill', which gave me a lead to look up the original material in the newspapers.

STREET DIRECTORIES

There are several different types of directories available:

- **Commercial directories** – these list merchants and traders.
- **Professional directories** – these list mainly the gentry, wealthy trades-people and professionals, and may list addresses, but not occupations.
- **General trade directories** – these list both 'private residents' and trades.
- **Specialist directories** – these list tradespeople in specific industries.
- **Town directories** – these list information only for one town or city rather than a county or part of a county (for example, *The Norwich Directory or Gentlemen and Tradesmen's Assistant*, printed by William Chase in March 1783).
- **National and provincial directories** – these covered several towns within a region, or perhaps a county, or even, in the case of the *Universal Directory* of 1793–8, the whole country.

You should be able to find copies of street directories at your local reference library; your local record office may also have a collection. Some directories are available on CD and have the added bonus of being searchable. Sections may be available on the internet, either via family history sites such as Genuki www.genuki.org.uk/, or projects such as the University of Leicester Historical Directories access project www.historicaldirectories.org. Copies of directories or facsimile reprints are available through second-hand and antiquarian booksellers, but can be a bit pricey.

Most of the larger directories (for example, *White's 1845 Norfolk*) contain general information about the county as a whole. These are worth sifting through as they might contain a reference to your particular building, particularly if you're researching a former school, workhouse or other institution.

This is also where it's useful to know the administrative district of the parish (see page 7 above), as some directories (such as *White's 1845 Norfolk*) list the towns within their Hundred division. Usually there's some statistical and general information about the Hundred and which union the parishes belong to. Then the towns and villages are listed in alphabetical order within the Hundred, each containing:

- a potted history;
- a note of important buildings, usually the church and schools;
- information about the post office and carriers;
- a list of 'private residents', i.e. clergy, gentry and some tradespeople;
- a list of tradespeople, sorted by trade.

There are a few problems you need to be aware of when working with directories:

- There are often gaps in a series of directories available at a library.
- Earlier directories aren't as detailed as later ones – for example, they might list a tradesperson, but wouldn't list a labourer or servant.
- The suburbs and villages tend to be less well covered than major cities and town centres, and entries for small towns and villages often don't include street names.
- Directories were prepared up to a year before publication, so the information might be out of date; other directories simply reprinted lists that were out of date.
- Details aren't always reliable – street numbering in particular can be a problem as it's either unreliable or missing, particularly before 1890.
- There are fewer directories available after the second world war, mainly due to the rise of free post office and, later, telephone directories.

Street directories tend to be more useful in tracing a business than in tracing individuals. I found them particularly useful when trying to track down the millers in Attleborough – and then again when I traced back the occupants of the cottage, using the census returns to help guide me. See Appendix 3 on page 187 and Appendix 4 on page 198 for examples of using directories to trace a particular occupation or the occupants of a house respectively.

The Architecture of Your House – External Features

This chapter deals with the architecture of your house and how it gives you clues to help you to date the property, including:

- clues about alterations to the building
- the house's plan and the materials of construction
- roof shapes, gables and parapets
- chimneys
- date stones
- boundaries
- outbuildings.

KEEPING IT IN CONTEXT

First you need to look at your house within its surroundings. Where is it built? Settlements usually spread outwards from the centre of the town, city or village, so if your house is near the middle it's likely to be older than houses on the outskirts unless, of course, the town has spread out far enough to encompass smaller, nearby villages. However, older properties are also more likely to have been rebuilt by a previous owner who either needed more space or wanted the property to look fashionable.

Look at the neighbouring houses too. Do they look similar? Are they from the same sort of date? Has the area been affected by the building of a railway or a bypass?

Simply looking at your house and the style in which it was built can help you give it a rough date. But there are some things you need to be wary about:

◆ Rebuilding or refacing – this may have been done in an architectural style that reflects an earlier or later date than that of the original building.
◆ Use of reclaimed materials – the building may have used material from an earlier property, though not necessarily from one that previously existed on the same site.
◆ 'Retro' styles were popular particularly in the nineteenth century, where different features from different periods were used in the same property. Towards the end of the century there was also a movement back to the original or 'vernacular' architecture of the particular region. The 1930s was also a period where mock-Tudor houses were built.

So it's always a good idea to look at the physical evidence side-by-side with documentary evidence, such as deeds, plans and maps, to make sure your house really is as old (or as new!) as you think.

Major architectural periods and styles

As a rough rule of thumb (with dates rounded up), these are:

Date	Period	Style
Up to 1480	Middle Ages	Medieval
1480–1550	Early Tudor	Tudor, early Renaissance
1550–1620	Late Tudor	Elizabethan, late Renaissance
1620–80	Stuart/Commonwealth	Jacobean, Baroque
1680–1750	William and Mary to George I	Early Georgian; neo-classical
1750–1810	Hanoverian	Late Georgian; neo-classical
1810–40	Regency and William IV	Regency; neo-classical

Date	Period	Style
1840–60	Victoria	Early Victorian (includes neo-Gothic)
1860–1900	Victoria	Late Victorian (including neo-Gothic, neo-classical, Arts and Crafts)
1900–20	Edward VII	Edwardian (includes Art Nouveau and early Modernist)

Alterations and additions

If you know that the house has been altered or built onto, think about why the changes were made. That can give you clues to the use of the house. This is particularly useful if your house used to be a shop, business or a pub – it means you'll have more sources for potential leads to research its history.

Pointers that could show your house has been altered include:

◆ Bricks on different walls being a different colour, shape or size.
◆ Decorative patterns being cut off abruptly.
◆ A line (known as a 'course') of narrow stonework or brick just above the lintels of windows; this may suggest that another storey has been added to the original building.
◆ Changes in the roofline (roofs of different pitches suggest an extension or refacing).
◆ Blocked-up openings of former doors and windows.
◆ Steps down to the entrance – this can point to the floor being lowered to give extra height to rooms, which was fashionable in the mid-seventeenth century. As a rule of thumb the lower the storeys (i.e. low internal ceilings), the older the building; if the ceilings have been raised or the roofline altered, you may also see evidence at the gable ends of the building.
◆ A symmetrical front except for the chimneys. A symmetrical frontage suggests that it dates from the end of the seventeenth century or later; but if the chimney stacks aren't also symmetrical it

suggests that the house is older. Although it was relatively easy to change the front of the house, moving the chimney stacks was more difficult and tended not to be done.

PLAN OF THE HOUSE

The earliest rural houses were long houses – that is, houses where the rooms were arranged in a row without a corridor. High-status houses had two storeys; the ground floor was used for storage and the top floor had an external staircase which led to a hall with a fireplace and a 'solar' (private living room). Lower status houses were single storey, with one or two bays for the animals, one or two bays for the living quarters, and a loft above the living quarters for sleeping. During Tudor times the byre was moved to a separate building and the space tended to be remodelled as a kitchen.

Medieval hall houses usually had a large open hall that was two storeys high and could be several bays long. At one end, near the entrance doors (partitioned by a wooden screen – known as a 'screens passage') were the service rooms, i.e. kitchen, pantry (where food was stored) and buttery (where liquids were stored); at the other end there would be a raised dais or platform where people ate and then the parlour, with stairs to a solar or bedroom. During Tudor times fireplaces were inserted in the centre and there tended to be one room on one side of the chimney stack and two on the other; a floor was inserted at first-floor height so the hall became single-storey and there was more accommodation on the top floor.

In towns, because space was limited, houses tended to be narrow with the gable end on the street and the main part of the house running back from it. The first room might be the craftsman's room or shop; behind that there would be a two-storey hall, and behind that would be store rooms. The kitchen would be at the other side of the courtyard, and the first floor rooms would be the living rooms and sleeping rooms. There might also be a cellar or undercroft, used for storage. As with the medieval hall houses, chimneys were inserted and the hall became single-storey to give additional accommodation.

By Georgian times houses tended to be built to a plan two rooms deep; the entrance hall led to the stairs (although in some houses the stairs were 'hidden' at the sides) and acted as a corridor leading to the kitchen, dining room and living rooms. Town houses were still long, but had an entrance hall acting as a corridor leading to the living rooms with stairs on one side of it.

Terraces developed during the eighteenth century, mainly for the well-to-do classes, but in the nineteenth century terraces were seen as working-class homes and were often built 'back to back'.

PHYSICAL ATTRIBUTES OF THE BUILDING
Construction – timber

Timber-framed houses usually have either a cruck frame or a box frame. The walls tend to be thinner than those of clay construction.

Crucks are two large curved timbers which make a triangle at each end of the house (a bit like a capital A), with a beam joining the pairs of crucks across the top to make the ridge of the roof; the crucks also form the walls of the building. The roof trusses were usually between 12 and 16 feet apart, and the space between them was known as a 'bay'.

Box frames have vertical posts with horizontal beams that make a box shape. The walls are usually made of the same material as the frame (known as a 'mass wall'), or additional beams make smaller panels within the frames that are filled in (known as a 'frame wall'). The box frames tended to be made up in the carpenter's yard to check that they fitted together properly, then each piece would be numbered before the frame was dismantled and put together in its final position. A good example of this 'prefab' timber-framed construction survives in Norwich; Augustine Steward's house (shown in picture 4.1 below) still has the numbers marked on the timbers.

The most common fillings for frame walls are wattle and daub (woven wood with a mixture of clay, dung and horsehair spread over it) and brickwork. Where you have exposed timbers externally, look at the distance between them. As a rule of thumb the smaller the gap between them, the more likely it is that the building was high status. Large square panels were common in the fourteenth and fifteenth centuries; smaller panels were more common in the sixteenth and seventeenth centuries.

4.1 Example of timber-framed house with daub infill – built in 1549 for Augustine Steward, the former Mayor of Norwich.

4.2 Example of seventeenth-century timber-framed house with herringbone brick infill and jettied upper floor.

Construction – brick

Bricks were expensive until the sixteenth century, so they tended to be used mainly for the houses of wealthy people. They were hand-made at first and their size wasn't regulated until 1571, when the legal standard size was set at 9 inches x 4.5 inches x 2.25 inches (229mm x 114mm x 57mm).

It's worth measuring the size of the bricks on your property because they can give you a clue about dating. In 1766 the legal standard size changed to 8.5 inches x 4 inches x 2.5 inches (216mm x 102mm x 64mm), and the legal standard size changed again in the 1960s to 215mm x 102.5mm x 65mm (8.5 inches x 4 inches x 2.5 inches). Smaller, irregular-shaped bricks are likely to be older than uniformly sized bricks, though it's worth remembering that sometimes bricks from older properties were reused in new buildings. Larger bricks suggest that the construction might be some time between 1784, when the first brick tax was introduced (the tax was made on the number of bricks used rather than the area of brickwork, so larger bricks meant a smaller tax payment) and 1803, when the larger bricks were taxed. The brick tax was repealed in 1850.

The colour of the bricks varies depending on where you are in the country, including various shades of red, creamy-yellow and blue-black. There may be local names for certain types of bricks, too; for example, the creamy-yellow brick in Suffolk is known as 'gault'. The colour also reflects building fashions:

- Red brick was fashionable in the sixteenth, seventeenth and early eighteenth century.
- Grey and brown bricks were fashionable in the mid to late eighteenth century.

- Grey, yellow and white bricks were fashionable in the late eighteenth and early nineteenth century.
- Red bricks became fashionable again in middle class houses in the late nineteenth century (when yellow bricks – 'London stock' – were seen as working class).

The pointing of the brickwork can also give you a clue to dates. Before the nineteenth century, bricks were sandwiched together with lime mortar; the sand in the mortar was quite coarse compared with modern brickwork. Though bear in mind that buildings are often repointed to prevent structural damage from weathering, so the clue might not be there.

The place you're most likely to find original brickwork is in a cellar, because walls can be refaced or rebuilt. It may be that the cellar is older than the rest of the building, for example if the house originally built over the cellar was knocked down and a new one built on the old cellar and foundations.

The way that bricks are laid is known as a bond. The three main types of bond are English bond, Flemish bond and stretcher bond; though you may also find 'random' bond, where no pattern is visible at all.

English bond has alternate courses of headers (the short horizontal side of the brick) and stretchers (the long horizontal side of the brick). This form of bond was popular between the middle of the sixteenth century and the beginning of the eighteenth century.

4.3 English bond.

Flemish bond is where all rows have alternating headers and stretchers; the headers are centred against the stretchers above and below them. This style of bond took over in the eighteenth century.

4.4 Flemish bond.

Stretcher bond (shown in picture 4.5) is where all bricks are stretchers; it became more popular in the nineteenth century when metal ties were introduced and bricks no longer needed to be laid as headers to bridge the gap between the internal and external wall.

However, these dates aren't quite 'set in brick' because more modern buildings often use retro features – the brickwork on picture 4.3 above is actually twenty-first century, not seventeenth!

4.5 Stretcher bond.

As well as the bonds and sizes of bricks used, there are two other things to notice on the brickwork: string courses and decorative patterns.

A string course is a long horizontal projecting course of bricks; it may be moulded (as in the example in picture 4.6 below), or in a different colour brick or laid in a different pattern. It's usually there for decorative purposes, although sometimes it can indicate that an extra storey has been added to the property or that the roof was raised slightly to give the ceiling extra height, particularly if the string course is very close to the top of a window.

4.6 Example of string course visible above ground floor level – Cotman House in Norwich.

You may also see patterns in brickwork, where different coloured bricks are used as contrast. The main ones are:

- Diapers – diamond-shaped patterns; these are also used on flint buildings to provide contrast.
- Chequerwork – where bricks are laid in alternate colours, much like a chequerboard. This was particularly used in the Tudor period.

You may also see a date or initials of a former owner laid in different colour bricks on the gable end of a house. As with dating stones, you need to be careful about how you interpret the date – it might refer to rebuilding or refacing rather than the original building.

Some bricks are shaped or glazed; round-cornered and glazed bricks are most likely to be found in Victorian and Edwardian properties.

Construction – cob and daub

Cob is a mixture of earth or clay and straw, laid in thick bands. It's usually rendered over with a lime plaster. If bricks or stone aren't used as quoins (corners), the walls may have rounded corners.

Clay lump (common to Norfolk) is a special form of cob made of clay and horsehair, set in a wooden frame to make oversized bricks (known as 'bats') which are then stuck together with mortar.

Wattle and daub is a similar method where upright stakes are bound together with withies (thin, flexible twigs – often willow) and then covered with daub, a mud-based filling that sometimes included straw, crushed or powdered chalk, sand and clay. The daub was put on to the wattle in wet handfuls (known as 'cats') on both sides of the wattle at the same time and pressed in. Once the daub had dried, it was covered in lime plaster.

Construction – stone and flint

The use of stone depends much on the local area; granite is used in Cornwall and the west, limestone in Dorset through to the north east, and sandstone throughout the country. Flint is commonly used in East Anglia and coastal regions; in high-status properties the flint is knapped (i.e. split and the flat edge is shaped into a square), whereas in cheaper properties it was left undressed.

4.7 Example of knapped flint, from the Bridewell at Norwich – formerly the house of the Appleyard family. The traveller Celia Fiennes, writing in 1698, described this as 'the finest piece of flintwork in England'.

Stone is sometimes used just for the quoins of a building, which is usually dressed stone laid so that there are alternately large and small faces. The use of stone quoins is a common feature of Georgian houses.

4.8 Quoins

Other external wall finishes

Apart from brick, stone and flint, the most common external finishes are render and stucco.

Render is a coating, usually rough. Popular types of render include:

- Lime plaster – often used to cover timber buildings. In the sixteenth and seventeenth centuries it was used in East Anglia to cover timbers and was called pargeting. Rather than being smooth, pargeting has regular patterns (combed work) or more complex moulded designs such as flowers, birds and motifs.
- Limewash – often used to cover flint or rubble walls, particularly if the stone was porous, as it helped with weatherproofing. In the nineteenth century it was fashionable to clean off the limewash. Both

limewash and lime plaster could be coloured; umber gave the plaster a brown or yellow finish, and bull's blood gave the pink finish seen commonly in East Anglia.

- Cement (used from the late eighteenth century), usually Liardet's, Parker's Roman, and Aspdin's Portland. Portland cement was used for stamped work in Victorian times, which copied the pargeting of centuries before.

- Stucco – this was a type of plaster with a smooth finish, which fell out of favour in the mid nineteenth-century. Sometimes stucco is coloured and 'grained' to look like ashlar stone, i.e. a dressed stone facing about 5cm thick that was put on the outside of load-bearing walls.

- Roughcast – a mixture of lime and gravel, commonly used from the 1850s.

- Pebble-dash – mortar mixed with smooth pebbles; this was used in the early twentieth century.

4.9 Example of moulded pargeting at Bishop Bonner's cottage in Dereham, Norfolk.

Terracotta plaques are often used to decorate Victorian and Edwardian buildings. In Norfolk anything apparently terracotta is more likely to be a special form of moulded brick, produced locally and known as Cosseyware. If the terracotta has been glazed, it's known as faience.

4.10 Example of terracotta plaques set within brickwork.

Glazed tiles are also very common in Victorian and Edwardian buildings.

Wall plates

If there has been a structural problem with the property you may see evidence that a metal tie has been inserted between two walls; the tie usually involves a metal cross, bar, S-shape or disc on the outside of the wall. The S-shaped tie is sometimes formed as a snake. (See picture 4.12 on page 47 for an example of metal ties on the gable end of a pitched roof.)

ROOF SHAPES, GABLES AND PARAPETS

Look at the rafters, which give the roof its shape, and their covering. Check for any changes to the roofline: this can show that the property has been extended. For rafters, the wider and shallower they are the older they're likely to be.

Although tales of timbers from shipwrecks being used for the structure of a house are very appealing, they're also likely to be colourful rather than true: wood used at sea would be seasoned and hardened, and therefore very difficult to use in a building.

The gable end can sometimes show if a building has been altered – for example, if the pitch of the roof has been flattened to give more headroom in the top storey you may see different building material in a triangular shape at the edge of the gable.

4.11 Changes to roofline visible at side of gable.

Roof shapes

A standard pitched (sloping) roof looks like a capital A from the gable at the side. As a rule of thumb earlier buildings tend to have a steeper pitch because it helped rain and snow fall off more quickly before it penetrated the roof covering. But beware of retro designs in more modern buildings: for example, what looks like a Tudor building may well be a 1930s 'retro' design.

4.12 Gable end of a pitched roof.

Where a house has been extended to a 'double pile' construction (two bays wide) you may see an M-shaped roof; this is more common from the eighteenth century. With double pile houses the main living rooms were at the front of the house, the bedrooms were on the first floor and the kitchen and servants' rooms were at the back.

4.13 Double-pile roof.

A hipped roof is where there's a slope to the ends of the roof as well as the sides. From the front it looks like a typical child's drawing of a house.

4.14 Hipped roof.

A Mansard roof is where the pitch (slope) of the roof changes halfway down; the top half is less steep than the bottom half. It first became popular in the mid-seventeenth century, mainly as a way of getting more 'headroom' in rooms that were used perhaps as servants' quarters.

4.15 Mansard roof.

A catslide roof is a pitched roof where the angle of the slope is the same at both sides of the ridge, but one side is longer than the other. It became popular in the late seventeenth century and was a way of getting more space in a small house, or moving servants' quarters to the back of the property. See pictures 5.14 and 5.15 of Mill House on pages 73 and 74 for an example of a catslide roof: the catslide goes over the bathroom (originally the back bedroom) and stairs, both of which have vaulted ceilings.

Gables

A gable is the vertical, triangular-shaped part of a pitched roof. They may be plain (as in picture 4.12 on page 47), or more decorative. Common decorative gables used from the seventeenth century are the Flemish or Dutch gable and the crow step or Corbie gable.

4.16 Flemish or Dutch gable.

4.17 Crow step or Corbie gable.

Parapets

In the eighteenth century rooflines, and their windows, which usually belonged to servants' quarters, tended to be hidden by low walls known as parapets.

4.18 Example of a parapet.

Ridges, finials, bargeboards and cornices

The ridge (top point) of the roof needs to be waterproofed, so there are special sorts of tiles which curve over the ridge. These may be plain or, particularly in Victorian houses, have an ornamental 'crest' that sticks up. (See picture 4.24 on page 55 for an example of an ornamental ridge.)

Finials are decorative ends to roof ridges or at the top of a gable; they're usually made from terracotta but may also be made from stone or iron. Again, they tend to be mainly Victorian.

Bargeboards are the wooden decoration on a gable (usually pitched). If they're very decorative they're likely to be mid-Victorian; by the Edwardian era bargeboards had become very plain again.

Cornices are ornamental projecting features on the walls just underneath the eaves (on internal walls they're known as coving). The two most common designs are:

◆ Dentilation – the headers jut out slightly with gaps between.

4.19 Example of a dentilation cornice.

◆ Dogtooth – the bricks are laid at an angle so the corners project.

4.20 Example of a dogtooth cornice.

You may also see very ornate cornices on late Victorian or Edwardian houses which are as ornate as those found internally; these tend to be made from white terracotta.

Roof coverings

Thatch was used from quite early on as a roof covering. However, because thatch needs replacing regularly, it's quite difficult to date a thatched roof.

There may be laws about the use of thatch in a town to give you some clues – for example, Norwich suffered severely from fires in 1507, so a law was passed forbidding the use of thatch as a roofing material for anything built after that. The five original thatched properties within the old city walls date from before those fires.

Thatch was sometimes replaced by tiles or slate; if the roof is very steeply pitched it's possible that the original roofing material was thatch. You may also see 'weatherings' – these are projecting courses of brick on chimney stacks or adjoining walls that are well above the later roof line, because a layer of thatch is obviously much thicker than a layer of tiles.

4.21 The Hermitage in Bishopsgate, Norwich – one of the five remaining original thatched houses in the city.

Shingles were flat 'tiles' made from thin slabs of oak. Stone and clay tiles were used from the sixteenth century onwards; these were either flat tiles made from stone or clay which were 'pegged' onto battens in an overlapping pattern, similar to shingles, or curved (S-shaped) pan-tiles made from clay.

Slate was a common roofing material in Wales. From the nineteenth century onwards, when transport links improved, it was used in other parts of the UK.

Lead flashing on tile and slate roofs were uncommon before the eighteenth century. Thatched houses didn't tend to have gutters or downpipes. The first downpipes and gutters were made from lead, or timber lined with lead, and may have dates on them as well as ornamentation, though it's possible that the building is earlier than the date inscribed on the rainwater head, particularly if the roof was originally thatched. In the nineteenth century cast iron guttering and downpipes began to be used; the square ones couldn't be painted at the back and tended to rust through, so circular downpipes were more practical.

CHIMNEYS

Looking at the chimney stacks may give you an idea of dating, but again, be aware of the possibility of replacement stacks or 'retro' building. Stacks from the early seventeenth century often have angled shafts.

4.22 Example of angled chimney shafts.

By 1650 these have become wider rectangular stacks with arched patterns, and by the eighteenth century the stacks are slightly splayed at the top. Late eighteenth century stacks may have string courses and cornices.

4.23 Example of an eighteenth-century chimney shaft with string course and cornice.

Fancy, ornate chimney stacks (often Tudor revival style) were very popular in Victorian houses.

4.24 Example of ornate chimney stack from house dating from 1849.

Look at the number of chimney stacks and relate them to the number of fireplaces within the property; this might help you if your property is old enough to have been subject to hearth taxes (see Chapter 8, pages 123–5).

Watch out for 'false' chimneys, which were built to give an illusion of wealth and don't actually relate to a hearth in the building. (The false stacks weren't taxed – the tax was based on the number of hearths rather than the number of chimney stacks.) In Mill House, shown in pictures 5.14 and 5.15 on pages 73 and 74, there are two chimney stacks with three chimney pots. Looking at them from the back of the house the left-hand one relates to the hearth in the living room; the two right-hand ones relate to the back-to-back hearths in the dining room and (formerly) kitchen.

DATE STONES, INSCRIPTIONS AND FIRE INSURANCE PLAQUES

Date stones may show the date of the building, but the date might refer to rebuilding, alterations, or even the commemoration of a marriage. It's more likely to refer to the date of the building if it's part of a structural stone such as a door lintel.

If there are initials or an owner's name inscribed next to the date, you may be able to trace that person through the parish registers (see Chapter 9).

Fire insurance plaques may help you trace the property through insurance records. The plaque will give you the name of the company that insured the building for fire; there should also be a number on the plaque, which is the policy number. If the insurance company or the company that took it over still has the records, you may find a description of the house and possibly even plans from the nineteenth century. However, be aware that these fire insurance plaques are often sold as antiques so the plaque on your house might have referred to a completely different building.

BOUNDARIES

Look at the boundaries of the property. Are they fenced, or are there brick or stone walls? A dry-stone wall is likely to be earlier than one finished with mortar.

Changes in the level of the garden may point to an earlier structure there, such as a well or a wall. It's also worth looking at modern boundaries to compare them with previous maps (see Chapter 6 for more details).

OUTHOUSES

Were any of the buildings used as an outside kitchen or toilet? For example, Mill House had an outbuilding that had been used as the scullery and contained a butler's sink. There was a section at the back of the outbuilding that was used as a coal hole (and I can just about remember the coalman delivering sacks of coal straight into the coal hole, in the years before we had central heating); there was also an outside toilet, set about 20 feet away from the house. You may find evidence in bundles of deeds about when a house was modernised with an inside bathroom and toilet or central heating.

5

The Architecture of Your House – Internal Features

This chapter deals with:

- the doors, windows and internal features of your house
- and how they can give you clues to help you to date the property.

DOORS

Has a door been moved? Look at the shape of the door and its surroundings. Are there any steps? This may hint that the door has been moved. In older properties you might even see where a door has been bricked up, in much the same way that you see bricked-up windows. In the mid-seventeenth century higher ceilings became fashionable, and the easiest way to raise the ceiling was to dig out the earthen floor – so steps going down to the front entrance may hint at a change like this. In the nineteenth century it was more fashionable to have a raised ground floor above a basement, with steps leading up to the front door.

Doors, windows and any ironwork (such as guttering) were usually painted the same colour; the finish tended to be matt or semi-gloss until the Edwardian period. Earlier doors weren't painted at all. Georgian doors and windows were usually painted black or dark green, while some eighteenth-century doors were painted bright blue.

Batten doors

The earliest doors were simple planked or 'batten' doors – that is, a row of vertical planks, with a series of planks fixed horizontally to the back of the door. There may be an arch on fifteenth- and sixteenth-century doors. As a rule of thumb the flatter the arch, the later the door. Doors from Tudor and earlier periods tend to be lower than modern doors, simply because people were shorter then. Some early doors are large enough for a man on horseback to ride through, and then a smaller door known as a 'wicket' door, big enough for someone to walk through, is cut into the door.

5.1 Example of batten door with 'wicket'.

Panelled doors

Panelled doors were introduced in the late 1500s and became more widespread in the 1600s. They tended to have square heads rather than arched. The earliest ones had two raised panels; by the eighteenth century six panels was the norm (see pictures 5.2 and 5.3 for examples).

By the mid-nineteenth century doors had four panels (the two longest ones at the top) with a rectangular window above them and by the end of the nineteenth century windows within doors (often stained glass) were fashionable.

Door surrounds

Tudor doorways often have stone or brick mouldings above the door – these were meant to stop rain falling down the wall onto the door. In the sixteenth and seventeenth centuries these mouldings became more geometrical, and by the 1750s doors started to have pediments and pilasters.

Pediments are low-pitched triangular gables over the top of a door; they became popular from the eighteenth century.

5.2 Example of a pediment.

Pilasters are flattened columns which frame doors or windows.

5.3 Example of pilasters.

Porticoes are where the entrance has columns supporting a roof.

5.4 Example of a portico.

In the eighteenth century fanlights above doors tended to have wooden glazing bars; wood didn't weather well, so the wooden glazing bars were often replaced by lead or wrought iron. Towards the end of the eighteenth century fanlights became mass-produced with designs such as spider-webs or loops (see picture 5.3 above). In the nineteenth century these became fancier still with flower or heart motifs.

Porches may be an addition to the property rather than an original feature. Early porches were simply lean-to roofs on brackets. By the eighteenth century they evolved into porticoes and pediments, and in the nineteenth century cast-iron or trellis porches were fashionable.

WINDOWS

Note how many windows there are. This may be useful if you're checking window tax records, though obviously if the house has been altered the number of windows may vary in the records. Are any of the windows bricked up? This might have been a way to avoid window tax, or it might simply show that the house was altered so the window was no longer needed. Georgian builders sometimes included 'fake' windows so the façade of the house would look symmetrical. An example of a bricked-up window is in picture 4.7 on page 43.

Look at the position and shape of the windows. If they're symmetrical on one side of the house, but are of a different shape or asymmetrical on the other side, the house may have been altered.

Medieval and Tudor windows tend to be rectangular with the longest edge horizontal. In the sixteenth and seventeenth centuries there was often a projected weather mould, known as a rainhood, hood mould or label mould, built over the top of the window.

5.5 Hood mould above mullioned window.

From the late seventeenth century vertical windows were more fashionable and medieval windows were sometimes ripped out and replaced. Whatever the age of the property, replacement windows may be more modern than the rest of the house.

Sash windows became popular in the late seventeenth and early eighteenth century. By 1820 the standard sash windows had 12 panes (i.e. two rows of three panes in each sash). Glazing bars became thinner between the seventeenth and nineteenth century.

Mullioned windows

Mullioned windows have a vertical bar known as a pier made of stone or wood which divides the opening into 'lights'. These tend to be the earliest type of windows, and the lights are narrow because of the way glass was produced (see page 68). In the earliest houses the windows were unglazed, or glazed with horn and draughts were kept out by shutters.

5.6 Mullioned window.

Casement windows

Casement windows are hinged either at the top or the bottom. They usually open outwards, though may open inwards. See picture 4.12 for an example of a casement window.

Sash windows

The earliest sash windows, from around the 1680s, didn't have pulleys; you simply pushed the window up and wedged it open. Boxes with pulleys, ropes and weights to hold the window open were introduced next. In 1709 there was legislation in London so that all windows in new properties had to be set back into the wall rather than being flush with it, to help avoid the spread of fire: this is sometimes referred to as 'rebating' the window from the brickwork. This legislation extended to the rest of the country in 1820, so the position of the sash (i.e. set flush to the window or set back about four inches) may help you with dating. Earlier sash windows tend to have wider glazing bars.

When sheet glass became more widely available from the mid-nineteenth century, the number of panes in sash windows tended to reduce from 12 to four. Because there were fewer glazing bars the windows were weaker, so by the 1800s sash windows had 'horns' projecting from the end of the vertical frames to make them stronger. By the twentieth century there was just one pane in each sash – one at the top and one at the bottom.

In picture 5.8 on page 66, of Garsett House, at the top you can see an example of sash windows set flush against the wall; the house dates from 1589. (Picture 5.4 on page 61 is also of Garsett House – the portico is an addition to the building rather than an original feature.)

Venetian windows

These are three-part windows, with a central archway flanked by two narrower rectangular windows. They were popular in the late seventeenth and early eighteenth century. They are also known as Palladian windows, after the sixteenth-century Italian architect Andrea Palladio.

5.7 Venetian window.

Oriel windows

Oriel windows project from the upper storey of a building. They are similar to a bay window, but are supported by brackets and don't go all the way down to the ground level. They're usually rectangular or half-cylindrical (i.e. like a bow window), and they were often placed over the entrance or gateway to the building. They were first used in the fifteenth century and were popular in Tudor and Gothic architecture; there was also a revival in the late nineteenth century.

5.8 Oriel window in Garsett House, Prince's Street, Norwich – note also that each floor is jettied out above the next, suggesting that the house is of timber-framed construction.

Dormer windows

Dormer windows are set into a small gable projecting from a sloping roof. Earlier dormers (from the mid-seventeenth century) are likely to be placed lower down the roof, resting on the eaves.

5.9 Carlton Terrace in Norwich, built in 1881 by Edward Skipper – the architect here was really showcasing his work, with dormer windows at the top, sash windows on the first floor and angled bay windows on the ground and basement floors.

Bay windows

Bay windows project out from the building and extend down to ground level. They can have angled sides, as in the windows in picture 5.9 above, straight sides, or, when the whole window is curved, it's known as a bow window. Bow windows were popular from the middle of the eighteenth century, especially in shops. In 1878 a building act stated that bay windows were not to extend more than 3 feet (about 90cm) from the front of the house, and they had to take up less than 60% of the house's frontage – so it could be worth measuring any bay windows in your property as an aid to dating the window, provided of course that the builder stuck to the rules!

GLASS

Look also at the panes of glass in the windows. Are they plate glass, are they stained or plain and are there any fanlights, i.e. panels just above a door?

Glass was made as cylinders (also known as 'broad glass') until the eighteenth century. The glass was blown into a sphere then stretched into a cylinder; the ends of the cylinder were removed, then the cylinder was slit and flattened out. The glass was then cut into small panes (set into square or diamond leads). Glass made in this way may look slightly green or grey and may have bubbles in it.

Crown or Normandy glass was produced next, where the glass was blown into a sphere, cut open, then spun against a wooden surface until it stretched. It was cut into squares once cooled and the 'bull's eye' at the centre was thrown out. The contemporary use of bull's eye glass reflects modern rather than period taste!

Mechanisation of the cylinder method meant that glass producers could make larger panes. Plate glass was also perfected by making thicker crown glass and then polishing it until the flaws had gone. Plate glass was developed in the 1830s and became more widespread from the mid-1800s onwards. This meant that older windows with smaller panes and more glazing bars were replaced by modern windows with large panes of glass.

Stained glass was popular in the early nineteenth century – particularly used in fanlights, front doors and hall windows – and remained popular until the 1930s.

INTERNAL FEATURES
Coving and skirting
Coving is the concave surface at the junction of a ceiling and wall; skirting is the wooden strip at the bottom of an internal wall. They both tend to be very ornate in mid-Victorian and high status houses.

Dado rails

These rails, made of wood, are roughly halfway up the walls; the lower part of the wall is often panelled. They were originally put up to protect the walls from furniture, which was arranged round edges of rooms in the eighteenth and nineteenth century. When furniture began to be grouped in the middle of the room, in Victorian times, the dado rails were seen as decorative. However, from about 1870 their use declined, and by the late 1800s they only tended to be put in areas where there was likely to be damage to the walls, such as halls and stairs, where servants might knock buckets of coal or water against the walls.

Picture rails

There were used mainly from the mid-1800s in rooms with higher ceilings; their function was to separate off a frieze on the wall. By the Edwardian period the picture rails had moved down to the level of the top of the door. In the 1920s and 1930s, the picture rails were often replaced by a narrow shelf that was used to display plates.

Mill House originally had high-level picture rails, however they may have been added after the house was built.

Fireplaces

Before the nineteenth century fireplaces tended to be open and there was a large gap between the grate which held the fire and the mouth of the chimney flue. Burning logs were held up by a pair of iron bars known as firedogs. With inglenook fireplaces, people took their chairs much closer to the fire and were able to avoid draughts. There may be bread ovens built into the wall, or a niche for the salt cupboard (stored near the fire to keep the contents dry). Open fireplaces had a revival in the 1860s when the Gothic style became fashionable.

5.10 Open fireplace.

By the early 1800s most fireplaces had a cast-iron hob grate. The coal was burned in the hob, and the ash fell through the front and bottom bars into the cavity below. Air flow couldn't be controlled, so the heating wasn't particularly efficient. However, they became popular again in the Queen Anne revival in the late 1800s. Cast-iron fireplaces were blackleaded: blacklead was spread thinly onto the surface and then polished to a sheen. The alternative was a coat of matt black paint followed by waxing.

5.11 Hob grate.

The register grate – sometimes known as the Rumford grate – was introduced in the nineteenth century; the angled cheeks (or sides) of the grate deflected heat into the room. They were normally made in one piece from cast iron, although tiled cheeks were fashionable between 1880 and 1900. There was also a moveable plate in the flue which helped to control air flow. As with hob grates, register grates were made of cast iron and were either blackleaded or painted and waxed.

5.12 Register grate.

The surround of the fire could be made from brick, stone, marble or slate. Slate was sometimes painted or enamelled to make it look like marble. Wood became more popular from around 1900.

The hearth itself tended to be made from stone, marble, slate or tile.

Flooring

The earliest floors were made of beaten earth, covered with rushes. From there, the floors may have been replaced by flagstones, and by the seventeenth century brick and tile floors were the norm. Timber floors are more likely to date from the eighteenth century.

Staircases

The earliest staircases were simply ladders. The next development was triangular-shaped blocks of wood that were nailed to long stretchers of timber, then set at an angle. Sometimes there was panelling on the open side.

As flooring was introduced at first-floor level into hall houses, newel stairs developed: these were spiral stairs set around a central post. They were normally inserted near a chimney stack, though some were built in special stair turrets.

During the seventeenth century frame stairs were introduced. These had treads and risers, and the dog-leg stair, which turned at 180 degrees at a half-landing, developed from there. These stairs tended to be 'closed string' – that is, the treads and risers were hidden behind the piece of wood supporting the stairs so they couldn't be seen from the side of the staircase. 'Cut-string' stairs developed during the late eighteenth century, where the treads projected from the piece of wood supporting the stairs and were visible from the side of the staircase.

5.13 Cut-string dog-leg stairs.

Balusters could be plain or decorated. Wooden barley-sugar balusters were popular throughout the eighteenth century, and wrought iron balusters were developed during the same period, becoming simple and very slender by the Regency period.

CASE STUDY: MILL HOUSE, ATTLEBOROUGH

Mill House is set back from the High Street along a narrow driveway. Its neighbours are two prefabricated pre-war bungalows and a telephone exchange; the latter was built in the 1970s on the site of the old stables. At the back of the plot, where there used to be an orchard, there is a modern housing development. So there are no clues to the house from the environment.

The house is made of brick, tile and slate, though some internal walls are clay lump. The windows and front door were replaced in the late 1990s, but the original windows at the front were sash windows with pulleys, with the windows set back rather than flush, and those at the side and back of the house were casement windows.

The symmetry of the front elevation hints at classical style, dating from the earlier half of the nineteenth century.

5.14 Front and side elevation of Mill House in 1999, photograph courtesy of Kissinger Estate Agency.

5.15 Back and side elevation of Mill House in 1986.

The side and back of the house are more of a puzzle. The windows are casement, rather than sash, and they're not quite symmetrically placed. The arches immediately above the windows at the side and back are of rubbed brick, whereas the arches above the ground-floor windows at the front of the house have a smooth stucco finish. The top left-hand window on the gable is lower than the right, reflecting the fact that the internal floor at the back of the house is lower than the front at both ground and first-floor level. The roof at the front of the house is tiled in slate, whereas the back is in clay pantile - and the front is actually a few inches wider than the back. Internally, the back of the house has lower ceilings and floors than the front.

It would be tempting to speculate that the back and front of the house were built at different times. However, the roof is of a well-known type (catslide - see page 49) and there is no evidence of any joins in the brickwork. Plus, if the back of the house was an addition, the only place the stairs could have been was in the downstairs hall, leading up at a very steep angle to the landing between the three bedrooms; when the wallpaper in the hall was stripped back to bare walls in the 1970s there was no sign of any studwork from former stairs.

My view is that the house was refaced at some point in the 1800s. The original roof at the front was probably clay pantile, but was changed to slate because slate was expensive and made the property appear 'grander'. Beneath the stucco voussoirs over the windows and door at the front it's entirely possible that there is rubbed brick, as there is at the side and back of the house: again, the slight refacing would have made the house seem grander to clients. The fact that the house is slightly wider at the front than at the back supports the view that the house was refaced.

It's also possible that part of the house was used as an office, either for the mill or for the stables. There is a stone at the front of the house on the corner nearest to the driveway, which may have been used as a mounting block for horse-riders.

6

The Building Itself: Maps, Photographs and Sketches

This chapter covers:

◆ the different sorts of maps and illustrations that can be used for tracing the history of a property.

It's always a good idea to work backwards from the present day, looking first at the 1910–15 valuation (or Domesday) maps, then the Ordnance Survey maps, tithe maps and enclosure maps, so you can work back from known landmarks.

Working backwards in this way can also help you to pin a rough date on your property – i.e. it's likely to have been built somewhere between the earliest map that shows your house and the next earliest map that doesn't show your house. Be careful when you're using maps, though; your house may be built on the site of an earlier property, so you'll need to confirm the details with other records (such as title deeds) to make sure you're looking at the same property. And, just to make things awkward, not all maps show all buildings.

One of the important things to think about with maps is who made it and what the purpose of the map was. The valuation maps of 1910–15 are very accurate because the survey was made for the purposes of taxation.

1910–15 VALUATION MAPS (DOMESDAY)

Under the Finance Act 1910, all properties in England and Wales were surveyed and valued. The idea was to levy a tax when the property was sold; the tax was 20% of the difference between the value of the land at the 'Domesday' survey and the value when the land was sold. Although the tax was repealed in 1920 (and there were exemptions anyway – on farmland which hadn't increased its agricultural value, or on land less than 50 acres) the records produced are very useful now to house historians.

As part of the survey, all landowners had to fill in a form, and there was a fine of £50 for not returning it (equivalent to nearly £3,400 in today's money – this gives an idea of the importance the government placed on the survey). The records from this survey are known as the Lloyd George 'Domesday' books, and there are two parts to the information:

◆ the record maps themselves;
◆ the field/valuation books.

Each property surveyed was called a 'hereditament'.

The valuation books and maps are kept in local record offices, and the field books are kept in the National Archives in Kew (in series IR58). The working maps are also in the National Archives. They're split by region:

◆ London is IR121;
◆ South East is IR124;
◆ Wessex is IR125;
◆ Central is IR126;
◆ Anglia is IR127;
◆ Western is IR128;
◆ West Midland is IR129;
◆ East Midland is IR130;

- Welsh is IR131;
- Liverpool is IR132;
- Manchester is IR133;
- Yorkshire is IR134;
- Northern is IR135.

Within each region there are up to 22 districts.

Not all records survive; some were destroyed during the Second World War.

Record maps

The record maps are based on Ordnance Survey maps, which were the largest scale and most recent edition available. The most common scale used was the 25-inch maps (25 inches to the mile), although even larger scales were used for towns. Two sets of maps are used:

- **Working plans** – these were used during the survey and contain notes about rights of way and ownership of property. The hereditament number was marked in red ink and the boundaries have a colour wash, usually red or green. The boundaries of income tax parishes are marked in yellow.
- **Record sheet plans** – these were marked up with the boundaries and reference numbers of the hereditaments and were kept in district valuation offices,

You'll need to check the map first to get the hereditament number of the property; without that, you're working pretty much in the dark. However, if you know the owners' and occupiers' names you may still be able to trace the property in the valuation books if the map isn't available.

To get the map reference relating to your property, you'll need to check on a map grid (available at your local record office) to see which series of maps are concerned. Every part of England and Wales has been given a reference on a grid; for example, the part of Norfolk containing Attleborough is covered by grid reference 85. You then convert that number to Roman numerals (so in our example it's LXXXV).

That grid area is then divided into 16 smaller rectangles, numbered from 1 to 16: to get the number for the map area you want, you count the rectangles from left to right, row by row, i.e.:

1	2	3	4
5	6	7	8
9	10	11	12
13	14	15	16

In the example above, Attleborough town centre was covered by square number 11, so I ordered the map reference LXXXV/11.

Frustratingly, the local record office's copy of the map hadn't survived, although the valuation book was available. Finding the hereditament number for Mill House might have meant a trip to the National Archives in Kew. You can search the catalogues in the National Archives online at www.nationalarchives.gov.uk/catalogue/search.asp, so I was able to confirm that the reference for the field book was IR 58/15499 and the reference for the map was IR 127/9/672. The online catalogue showed that the map and the field books were held at Kew, so if I needed to I could order the documents before going to visit the archives.

Luckily, I was saved the trip to London because I already knew the owner's and occupier's names from other records (the deeds, the rate book and a sale catalogue), so I was able to look at the valuation book in my local record office and find the relevant record.

Field books

The field book records the details of the hereditament; the amount of details given varies between books, but could include:

- Full street address.
- Interior and exterior description: number and use of rooms, state of repair, date it was built and materials used, whether it has electricity or running water, and possibly a detailed plan of the building; may also describe gardens, outbuildings, outdoor sanitary arrangements (known as ECs or earth closets) and chicken runs. Industrial properties (mills, factories, shops and offices), schools and stations may be described in great detail, including cellars, fire escapes and storage areas.
- Name of owner.
- Name of occupier.
- Date of previous sales.
- Valuation figures.
- Schedule of neighbouring lands owned.
- Rents.
- Who paid rates, taxes and insurance.
- Who was liable for repairs.

At the end of a parish, public buildings and common land (such as parks and historic sites) are grouped together.

The earlier assessments tend to be much more detailed than the later ones, basically because the project fell behind schedule and then corners were cut to finish the assessments on time.

Valuation books

The valuation books (known as Domesday Books) were records of the hereditaments made from the field books; they don't contain the descriptions or plans of land and property, but can be useful in finding the hereditament number when the map hasn't survived (as happened in the case of my research). They're listed in parish order within income tax parishes. They list the owner, occupier, usage and extent of each hereditament in the parish, together with the hereditament number and map reference number.

From the field book I was able to see that the valuation was carried out between January and April 1913. Hereditament number 139 is very simply described as 'House and Garden in Mill Yard'; the occupier is William M. Gathergood and the owner is Anna Wright of Woodbridge. This tallied with the other documents I had.

The valuer estimated the extent of the land as 1275 square yards; the original gross value of the property was estimated at £361, of which £272 relates to the buildings. The property was described as having seven fruit trees (from my childhood I can remember that one was an apple tree – my father fixed a swing to one of the boughs) and flower borders.

ORDNANCE SURVEY MAPS

The Ordnance Survey was established in 1791; its function was to produce maps of Kent, Surrey and Sussex to help the military commanders prepare to repel French invaders. The first official map was produced in 1801.

After the war with France ended in 1815 the Board of Ordnance continued and expanded the maps to cover the rest of the country. Although Christopher and John Greenwood also started publishing 1-inch county maps in the 1820s, they abandoned the project when the Ordnance Survey project developed.

There were several editions of the Ordnance Survey maps:

◆ Old Series (which was completed in 1870). These were 1-inch maps (i.e. the scale was 1 inch to the mile) and the maps are basically a survey of the land.

- Second edition (also known as the 'New Series', which was started in 1870). These had three different scales:
  - 1 inch (i.e. one inch to the mile);
  - 6 inches (i.e. six inches to the mile);
  - 25 inches (i.e. extremely detailed, 25 inches to the mile – this tends to be for London and the larger towns). The 25-inch map shows railway lines, the shape and size of buildings, boundaries of fields and acreage sizes; it may also give house names, show the garden layout (including ponds), the number of seats in churches, the position of pillar boxes, lamp posts and horse troughs, and the width of pavements.
- Third edition (revised versions of the 6-inch and 25-inch maps) for some areas in 1900 and 1920.
- Fourth edition (for some areas) just before World War Two.

Most libraries and record offices have copies of the 1-inch maps through to the 25-inch maps. There are excellent collections at the National Archives and the British Library. There may also be some earlier maps online, depending on your county's archive. For example, Norfolk has digitised copies of various maps (including aerial photography) at www.historic-maps.norfolk.gov.uk/ and East Sussex has pre-1813 maps at www.envf.port.ac.uk/geo/research/historical/webmap/sussexmap/sussex.html.

Note that the maps might show the existence of larger individual large properties, but smaller houses are not necessarily shown.

Mill House is shown on both the Old Series (1838) and the Second Edition (1883) Ordnance Survey map covering Attleborough.

6.1 Section from the 1-inch Ordnance Survey map, 1st edition, 1838. Reproduced by kind permission of Ordnance Survey © Crown Copyright 1838. Mill House, with the mill, is just to the left of the circular road system.

6.2 Section from the 6-inch Ordnance Survey Map, 2nd edition, 1884. Reproduced by kind permission of Ordnance Survey © Crown Copyright 1884. Mill House is the L-shaped building above and slightly to the left of the letter W. The mill isn't actually marked as such on the map (and I know from trade directories that the mill was no longer working by then), but it could be the oblong building to the right of the world 'Mill' – the building immediately below that was the old stable complex.

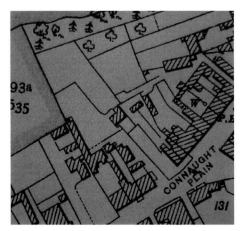

6.3 Section from the 25-inch Ordnance Survey Map, 1906. Reproduced by kind permission of Ordnance Survey © Crown Copyright 1906. Mill House is the L-shaped building at the end of the driveway (one side of the driveway is visible as a line showing the site boundary – the other end of that line is just above the letter O in 'Connaught Plain'. All traces of the mill are completely gone, though the stable block is still there to the left of the house.

This ties in with both the census returns (see pages 135–8) and the information in the street directories (see Appendix 3), which show that the mill had more or less ceased to function from around 1850. This is shortly after the railway came to the town and a new mill was built near the railway – so the reason for the mill's decline are obvious. The stables were, however, used until at least 1912, when the tenant of the house is described in a trade directory as a 'jobmaster' for the stables. The buildings were still there, albeit derelict, when my family moved to Mill House in 1969.

TITHE APPORTIONMENTS AND MAPS

In England a 'tithe' was paid to the church from early medieval times. The tithe itself was a tenth of the produce of the land – hay, wool, corn, fruit and the like. A third of the tithe (known as the 'small tithe') went to the vicar or deputy who served the church, and the remainder (known as the 'great tithe') went to the rector or the religious house that ruled the church. The tithe was meant to pay for the living of the parish priest.

After the dissolution of the monasteries the rights to tithes passed into private hands. When lands were enclosed, tithe owners were often given allotments of land in compensation. Tithe owners (including churches) might also agree to exchange a payment in kind for payment in cash. If cash was paid instead of produce, this was known as commutation.

In 1836 the Tithe Commutation Act converted the tithe from a payment in kind to a 'rent charge', which was paid to the local church. The actual amount of the rent charge varied; it depended on the way the land was cultivated and the price of corn. The Tithe Commission was set up in London and sent assistant commissioners to implement the Act in England and Wales; the implementation was made between 1836 and about 1850. In order to work out the award, the commissioners had to commission surveys of the land, then meet with the landowners and tithe owners and draw up a provisional agreement of the rent charge. If there was any disagreement the commissioners would have to arbitrate and work out an award. Once the agreement or award was confirmed one copy was kept in the parish chest, one was given to the bishop of the diocese and one remained with the Tithe Commission.

As part of the survey work, tithe maps were made. The scale of the maps was between 12 and 25 inches to the mile and the maps cover the whole parish. They show:

♦ boundaries, including early medieval parish boundaries, tithe-free monastic land and areas not yet enclosed, also field boundaries with hedges, fences, stiles and gates;

- buildings: on colour maps, inhabited buildings such as farmhouses and cottages are marked in red and other structures are marked in grey, on a monochrome map the inhabited buildings are shaded fully and the uninhabited buildings are cross-hatched;
- place names;
- compass bearings – note that north isn't necessarily at the top of the page.

Other features that may be shown on the map, depending on who made it, are:

- roads, turnpikes and toll houses;
- rivers, ponds and other bodies of water;
- railway lines;
- mills, factories, quarries, chalk pits and mines;
- woodlands;
- ice houses, dovecotes and lighthouses.

Note that the tithe map isn't necessarily an accurate survey of the area in the way that the 1910 survey and Ordnance Survey maps are. The purpose of the tithe maps was to show the boundaries of areas owing tithes, so sometimes buildings have been missed off maps completely (see below for the example of Mill House).

There was a full written schedule (or 'apportionment') with each map, describing the land, and field names were sometimes included. The schedule was arranged in alphabetic order of the landowner, and tenants are listed alphabetically underneath the landowner's name. Institutes (such as a turnpike trust, a chapel trustee and the parish) are listed at the end of the schedule. The apportionments generally show the following.

- Summary information of the parish: total area, name of tithe owner(s), acreage of titheable and non-titheable lands and information about lands that were exempt from tithes.

- Name of landowner, first and surname.
- Name of occupier, first and surname: may be 'himself' if the occupier is also the landowner, and in some cases the very tantalising comment 'and others' – particularly where tenants are concerned.
- Plot number: you can match this to the map.
- Name and description of land and premises: this includes field names, which are not shown on Ordnance Survey maps.
- State of cultivation, e.g. arable, pasture, rough grazing, marshland, timber, orchard, garden, hop field, market garden, meadow, coppice, paddock; however the type of crop isn't always shown, nor the type of livestock.
- Extent of land in acres, roods and perches – there were 40 perches in a rood, and 4 roods in an acre.
- Amount of rent charge payable.
- Remarks, e.g. if the plots became 'altered apportionments', which usually happened when a railway was built.
- Summary of schedule listing the landowners in alphabetical order, occupiers in order of amount of land held, and total of rent charge from each owner to each tithe owner.

There is a complete set of tithe maps at the National Archives in section IR30 and apportionments in IR29; you should also find the diocesan and/or parish copy of the maps at your local record office. All of the Welsh apportionments and most of the English ones are in microform. There is also some correspondence and copies of reports in series IR18.

Although they survive for almost all parishes, the maps vary in size, scale and accuracy – some give only the basics whereas others are much more detailed. Some of the maps are 14 feet square – they come in a roll, so you'll need to book a map table at the record office to look at them and also use weights to hold them open. Any amendments will be shown on a linen-backed Ordnance Survey map (usually the 6-inch format).

6.4 The Tithe Map for Attleborough, here shown held open by weights. Map held in Norfolk Record Office, reference NRO DN/TA84 – photograph by author, used by kind permission of Norfolk Record Office.

The apportionment books are usually rolled up inside the tithe map (along with the amendments) and again you'll need to use weights to hold the pages open. The parcel numbers of the land are not arranged numerically in the schedule, so you'll have to look through the book to find the exact plot you want.

The maps and apportionments are too large to copy on an A3 photocopier; as the books are bound and fairly fragile, you won't be able to copy them on a plan-printer either. Alternatives are photographing the books/map (though this depends on your record office's policies) or transcribing the details of the map onto a photocopy of a 6-inch Ordnance Survey map.

Most of the maps and apportionments date from the 1840s, so you should be able to cross-refer the information with census returns and possibly also with street directories.

The diocesan copy of the tithe map for Attleborough is in the Norfolk Record Office. Because it's a diocesan copy, the reference for the original map and apportionment is in series DN/TA (which stands for Diocesan Tithe Assessment). The document number in this case is 84.

Mill House is shown on plot 213, which is described as an 'orchard' and 'pasture' belonging to William Stannard Cockell. The area is described as 1 rood and 38 perches; next door, plot 212 is a paddock of 2 roods and 25 perches. The occupier of the land is 'John Mann and others', and it's described as 'cottages, Mill Yard and Garden'; the land is described as arable, with an area of 5 roods and 21 perches.

6.5 Section of Tithe Apportionment book for Attleborough showing the owner and occupant of Mill House (plot 213), held in Norfolk Record Office, reference NRO DN/TA84 – photograph by author, used by kind permission of Norfolk Record Office.

6.6 Section of Tithe Map for Attleborough, held in Norfolk Record Office, reference NRO DN/TA84 – photograph by author, used by kind permission of Norfolk Record Office.

In the above section we can see plot 213 quite clearly. The tithe map dates from 1838, the same date as the first Ordnance Survey map, although the detail of the buildings shown is quite different. This is because the tithe surveyors were more interested in boundaries than in actual buildings, and the Ordnance Survey cartographers were trying to make as accurate a record of the land and buildings as possible.

The W-shaped building at the front of the map is shaded red (occupied), and the two square-ish buildings are shaded grey (uninhabited).

It's possible that the top left-hand building on plot 213 represents the stable complex. The house doesn't appear at all and I would expect it to appear roughly by the number 3 of '213' – in the present day there's a narrow unpaved lane that runs along the top boundary of plot 212. The right-hand building is 'unoccupied'; there's a possibility this is the mill, but there isn't enough supporting detail for us to be sure.

ENCLOSURE MAPS AND AWARDS

Until the eighteenth century cultivation of land was based on the 'open field' system, where people had strips in each field and rights over common pasture and woodlands – 'common' land was actually owned privately, but people had 'rights of common' so they could let their animals graze over it.

Enclosure took place when these open fields and commons were converted to individual plots of private land, often with a fence or hedge put round it to separate it from a neighbour's land. The first agreements were made privately, between a landowner and tenants. Later they were subject to an Act of Parliament.

Sometimes common land was divided between freeholders in a manor, and sometimes arable land was rearranged so that farmers who had several strips of land in different large open fields would be given a single larger piece of land instead (equivalent to the same amount of land as the smaller pieces added together). These plots were called 'allotments' and they ranged in size from a small parcel to several hundred acres.

From the 1780s onwards a map of the land was included in an enclosure award.

The clerk of the peace collected the awards before 1792. After that, the awards had to be included ('enrolled') in records of the quarter sessions. There were also notifications in the local newspapers.

The Enclosure Commission was established in 1845. After then a central government department held a copy of all enclosure awards. The enclosure procedure also changed. Instead of needing an individual Act of Parliament for each enclosure, people simply applied to the Commission. The Commission assessed all the applications once a year and, if they were successful, they were actioned together.

There is no set format for enclosure awards, but they usually consist of a map and a schedule. The detail given on the maps is variable; it may show a map of the entire parish with its existing layout, and the proposals for enclosure superimposed on it. Sometimes it shows land ownership, roads, footpaths and boundaries. It may show who owned land, who bought it and how the land was affected by enclosure. The scale of the map is usually between 5 and 8 chains to the inch (39.6m to 63.36m to the centimetre), though occasionally smaller or larger scales are shown.

The number on each plot of land matches the number on the schedule, which will give:

◆ the landowner's name;
◆ the extent of holdings;
◆ the nature of tenure (freehold or copyhold).

The schedule may also list rights of way and say who was responsible for maintaining boundaries.

Local record offices usually have copies of the enclosure awards. Some awards after 1845 are held in the National Archives, series MAF1. There is also correspondence about enclosures (including information about disputes) in series MAF25.

Not all parishes have enclosure maps. The maps may not cover the entire parish – and note that 'enclosure' is also spelt 'inclosure' in some areas (such as Norfolk), so bear that in mind when looking up the records – particularly in an online catalogue.

For Attleborough the Inclosure Award dates from 1812. The map of 1815 is somewhat faded, but a certified copy of it was made by a draughtsman in 1930, at a scale of 1 inch to 8 chains. I was delighted to discover that this version of the map contained an inset detail of Attleborough town, at a scale of 1 inch to 3 chains. This map gave much more detail about who owned the land and how much land was in each parcel. This map shows clearly that the occupier of the land (equivalent to plots 212 and 213 on the tithe map) is Jonathan Cooper; the land is bounded by the street known as Levell Street or High Street on the left (as you look at the map), Connaught Plain in the middle (the triangular area) and Exchange Street heading up to the right-hand corner.

Again, the map doesn't actually show the house or the mill – which is strange, as other sources show that the house and mill existed there in at least 1804. The site of Mill House is roughly where the N of 'Jonathan' finishes; the larger rectangular dark-shaded (uninhabited) building above the light-shaded W-shaped building is the stable block.

6.7 Section of the inset detail from 1930 copy of enclosure map dated 1815, held in Norfolk Record Office, reference NRO C/Sca 2/10 – photograph by author, used by kind permission of Norfolk Record Office.

ROAD ORDER MAPS

If roads or footpaths were closed ('stopped up') or diverted as part of an Enclosure Act, there may be a road order map available, which will give details such as the name of the road or path affected, and may even show field names. Even though the Enclosure Act was the reason the road orders were made in these sort of cases, the road order map and its supporting documents will usually be separate from the Enclosure Act. The map may not be particularly detailed where buildings or rivers are concerned, as its primary function was to show footpaths and roads. A comparison of the areas shown in 6.7 above and 6.8 below, dated within two years of each other, illustrates just how much the surveyor ignored on one of these plans.

The supporting documentation will go through every single road and footpath on the map (they're often numbered rather than named) and will state exactly where they are and which direction they go in. The road order may also refer to the land surrounding the path and who owned it.

The road order map for Attleborough is entitled 'Stoppage of Highways and Footways, relative to Inclosures Act of 52 Geo. III' – in other words, the 52nd year of George III's reign, or somewhere between 25 October 1811 and 24 October 1812. This map clearly shows 'Mill Field' and 'Mill Piece'. According to the supporting documentation, Mill Piece was owned by Stephen Nobbs Stevens (whose name is mentioned in a news-paper advertisement for the mill in 1804), and Mill Field was owned by William Stannard Cockell (who was listed as the owner of plot 589 – equating to the Mill Field – on the tithe map shown in 6.6 above).

One problem with this type of plan is that they're folded into neat parcels – and if they haven't been opened for the best part of 200 years you'll have to peer into the creases (which are rather obvious on the pic-ture below) as the documents are too fragile to be flattened out completely. You may also find that a seal has stuck two parts of a piece of parchment together, so you might not be able to read the document in its entirety. If you're in this position, talk to the archive specialist – it goes without saying that you can't just rip the seal from the parchment!

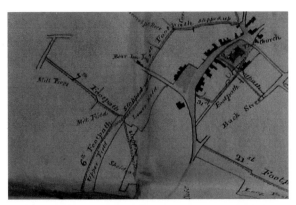

6.8 Detail from plan of the Stoppage of Highways and Footways dated 1812, held in Norfolk Record Office, reference NRO C/Sce 2/4/12 – pho-tograph by author, used by kind permission of Norfolk Record Office.

TOWN PLANS

Town plans tend to be produced from late 1500s and show the layout of the streets, including street names. Many more were produced in the nineteenth century as towns expanded. They were paid for by subscription, so whether one exists in your area really depends on whether enough people wanted a map and paid for it. Copies are likely to be in local record offices. There are also collections at the British Library and some in the London Metropolitan Archives.

There is no set format for town plans. Obviously, from the name, they are plans of a town. Street names will be marked, as well as local public buildings such as churches, workhouses, almshouses and hospitals, town halls, castles, gaols and lunatic asylums. The maps may show the buildings in great detail, they may also list subscribers' names.

Although there is a plan of Attleborough dating from the early 1800s, it is specific to one person's landholdings and doesn't show much of the town itself.

OTHER MAPS

Early maps tend to be funded by subscription from wealthy patrons. In Norfolk we're lucky to have two such maps covering the county: Faden's Map of 1797 and Bryant's Map of 1826.

In the section from Faden's map (6.9), there is a mill shown at Fettle Bridge Common (an area later known as Dodd's Road – named after the long-standing miller, Thomas Dodd), and a mill in the town centre (which was the mill near Mill House). The mill is shown slightly to the north of its actual position, due to the lettering on the map – it should be smack in the middle of the H in 'Attleborough'.

There is the possibility that this map shows the site of an earlier mill – the one connected with Mill House was built in 1804. Was the 1804 mill built on the site of the earlier one, or did it replace it? And what happened to the original mill? When was it demolished?

6.9 Detail from Map of Norfolk by William Faden, 1797, held in Norfolk Record Office, reference NRO PD 101/52 – photograph by author, used by kind permission of Norfolk Record Office.

There is also a slightly more detailed map of the county by Bryant, dating from 1826. The mill in the town centre is shown there, as well as Dodd's Mill and a third mill on Rivett's Lane, shown as 'World's End Lane' on the map in 6.9.

USING MAPS

You need to be aware of copyright law, especially if you're considering publishing your material. If a map was first published up to 50 years ago, it is still in copyright. You may be able to copy one A4 segment for your personal use, but check with the library or archive staff first. You may need to sign a copyright declaration form and have your photocopy stamped.

Some maps may be too large or fragile to be copied on an A3 or plan copier – particularly older maps. You may be able to photograph the maps – check with archive staff – or a facsimile or digitised version may be available. Tracing is another possibility, though you'll need to use clear plastic film between the map and the tracing paper to avoid damaging the map.

In all cases, if you're looking to publish any section of a map always check with the archive staff. They will advise you if copyright permission is needed and how to get it. If it's a matter of taking photographs, you will need to complete a permissions form and you may need a photograph permit to go with the form. Your local record office staff will be able to advise you about the procedures and guidelines in your area. The archive staff may also be able to suggest other sources to help you in your research, and if there is more than one edition of a map they will be able to tell you which is the one most likely to suit your needs.

SKETCHES

Sketches of the property may exist. For example, in Norwich the artist Henry Ninham made sketches of many buildings in the city, including the gates in the city wall which no longer exist. If your building is particularly interesting from an artist's point of view there may well be a sketch of it by a local artist and it's worth asking your local record office, museum or archive if they have any sketches on record.

PHOTOGRAPHS

There are many books of old photographs covering various towns and counties; your property may be shown there. However, if you want to use the photograph for publication, you'll need permission to use it. The best way to obtain permission is to contact the publisher and ask who holds the copyright.

Your county library may also hold a collection of photographs. Some may also be available online or in a digital format. For example, Norfolk County Council has a searchable picture library called Picture Norfolk, and you can purchase copies of the photographs.

If your building was involved in any particular event, such as a fire, flood, or was lived in by someone who hit the headlines, your local newspaper may have archive photographs or engravings/woodcuts of the event, kept in a private library. There is normally a charge to access a newspaper's photographic archives and you may also be able to purchase a copy of photographs. However, note that if you wish to use them for publication you'll need permission from the copyright holder.

English Heritage also has a large collection of photographs. There are searchable databases of them at their websites Images of England: www.imagesofengland.org.uk/ and Viewfinder: http://viewfinder. english-heritage.org.uk. Again, as with newspaper photographs, you'll need permission from the copyright holder if you wish to publish the photographs.

Unfortunately, I could find no trace of Mill House or the mill in sketches or old photographs of the town.

7

The Building Itself: Other Documents

This chapter looks at:

♦ other types of documents which can tell you about a property, such as sales particulars, newspaper advertisements, deposited plans, building control plans and planning applications
♦ and sources for buildings such as former schools, pubs and tollhouses.

SALES PARTICULARS

Sales particulars vary in the level of details they give. At the very least they will tell you where and when the sale of properties took place, right down to the time of day. The detailed particulars might include plans, any conditions for sale and details of the properties involved. If you have access to the deeds, it's worth cross-referencing the sale particulars to the deeds – you may be able to confirm details of the property that aren't shown in the deeds.

One of the properties in the sale referred to in the particulars below was Mill House. It was part of a sale which included 'three capital shops with dwelling houses in the main street, eight dwelling houses & villa residences, two public houses, four eligible buildings sites, two enclosures of Accommodation Arable and Pasture Land, fifty-seven cottages,

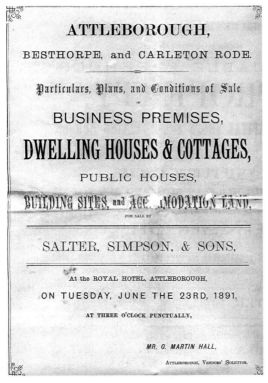

7.1 Front of sale particulars from the Wright Estate in Attleborough, 1891.

all situate in Attleborough' as well as 13 cottages in neighbouring villages. These were sold in 30 lots through the auctioneers Salter, Simpson and Sons.

The other photocopy from those particulars shows a detailed map of the lots involved (part of which was copied over to an indenture – see picture 8.1 on page 115). Sadly, the other side of the plan refers only to the first three lots (and Mill House was lot five). The detail is minute, though, and invaluable to the house historian. For example, the particulars for lot one are:

Coloured Light Blue on Plan No. 2:
a Red Brick and Tiled Dwelling House
with
Fishmonger's Shop,
Sitting Room, Storeroom, Scullery, with Pump and Four Bedrooms;
in the rear
Yard, Wash-house, Stable, Hay House with Loft above, Cart Shed,
Drying House, w.c., also detached a Piece of Ground, 13ft. 6in. long, x
7ft. 6in. wide, as coloured blue on plan
well situate in the Main Street
and abutting on right of way, and Lot 2; in the occupation of Mr. James
Johnson, at the Annual Rent of £11 15s. 0d.
Tithe   ..   ..   ..
Land Tax (if any)   ..   ..   ..
This lot has a right of way for Horses, Carriages and Stock over road
coloured light brown, paying a proportionate amount of keeping the
same in repair,
No Building, erection or addition shall be made beyond the present
frontage of this Lot.
The Double Doors, and Shop Fixtures are the property of Tenant.

NEWSPAPER ADVERTISEMENTS

Sales particulars such as those above might also be listed in newspapers, and again it's worth cross-referring to the deeds. Sometimes even more detail is given; or you may find a reference to the property that dates from before the deeds you've already seen. During my researches I was lucky enough to come across a really choice find in the *Norfolk Chronicle and Norwich Gazette*, dated 21 July 1804, reproduced below with original punctuation:

TO MILLERS

TO BE SOLD BY AUCTION,

Early in next month, unless previously disposed of by Private Contract,
A Very desirable ESTATE, pleasantly situate in the Town-street, in
Attleburgh, in Norfolk; comprising a capital new-erected tower built
Windmill, containing 6 floors, two pairs of French Stones, of $4\frac{1}{2}$ feet,
and one pair of 4 feet, cylinder and flour mill complete. – the ground
floor contains a horse-wheel, appendant to flour mill, winds herself,
draws 10 yards of cloth, the stage 22 feet from the ground, the whole
fitted up in the most complete manner, and in excellent repair. – A
brick and tiled Dwelling-house, replete with every convenience,
granary, stables, cart-sheds, piggeries, yards and garden, with suitable
offices, in excellent condition, with about two acres of land adjoining.
Possession of the whole may be had at Michaelmas. Land-tax
redeemed – All Freehold, except one acre of land, and has unlimited
rights on the rich commons of Attleburgh aforesaid.

N.B. The purchaser may be accommodated with the hire of about 8
acres of land.

The reason why Mr. Stevens sells the above is, he has taken a large
business in the farming line.

For particulars apply to Mr. S. N. Stevens, the Proprietor, or of Mr. N.
Lock, Millwright, Norwich.

The advertisement was repeated in the *Norfolk Chronicle and Norwich Gazette* on 4 August, this time with the additional detail that the sale would be by William Parson 'On Thursday the 9th of August, at four o'clock, at the Bear, in Attleburgh, Norfolk'.

I had thought that the house dated from the mid 1820s, so I was surprised to discover it was older than it looked. It was also interesting to see such full details of the mill and the cottage – we'd had no idea about presence of the piggeries and granary – and it confirmed my suspicion that the original roof was entirely tile rather than tile and slate.

DEPOSITED PLANS

From 1792 if you wanted to build a canal, turnpike, railway or dock, you had to deposit plans with the clerk of the peace as part of your building application. These are usually found in local record offices. They tend to be plans of public undertakings such as railways, but will often give details of who owned and occupied the land in the immediate vicinity of the railway, turnpike or other scheme.

The plans tend to be 'strip maps' – that is, a map of the strip of land. There is sometimes a book of reference that goes with the map, showing details of the land adjacent to the planned scheme. The details may include the size of the land in acres, roods and perches, who owned it, who occupied it and how the land was used, e.g. pasture, orchard, common land.

The amount of detail given in deposited plans really varies. Those for the railways tend to be very detailed, though it's worth noting that often the plans submitted by railway companies were never actually carried out.

BUILDING CONTROL PLANS

Before 1948 plans for new buildings or alterations to existing buildings had to be submitted to the local borough and district council for building control. The plans usually show a site map, plus elevations and sections of the building. They are available in local council planning archives or record offices. However, the survival of the plans can be patchy.

PRIVATE ESTATE MAPS

Between the end of the sixteenth century and the middle of the nineteenth century, estates produced maps of the property with a 'terrier' (or book) listing tenants and holdings. The terriers may mention the owners of adjoining properties, and may describe the acreage of the land and what it was used for. It may also detail property on the land (such as barns and cottages), woods, roads, paths and water. You may also find rent rolls – schedules listing tenants, rents paid/due, description of land and buildings. Maps may contain drawings such as of churches and manor houses.

Some maps are available at local record offices. However, they haven't survived for all parishes and if they haven't been deposited at the record office they may still be in private hands.

SPECIALIST BUILDINGS
Former pubs

If your house was a former public house you may find more information about former occupiers (the licensees) and pub names in the registers of licensed victuallers.

Taverns and inns had to be licensed. JPs issued licenses, often with a bond of surety (sometimes called recognizances) for the orderly keeping of the house and these licenses were kept in registers of licensed victuallers. The records should tell you:

- the name of the licensee;
- the parish in which the pub was situated;
- the name of the person standing surety;
- the name of the alehouse, tavern or inn.

Licensing legislation changed between 1828 and 1869 so records and registers didn't have to be kept. A new licensing system was brought in from 1869 and registers of licenses were kept from 1872.

These registers are usually held in local record offices and you'll find them among the Quarter Sessions Records (often referred to as Q/RLV, i.e. Quarter sessions Register of Licensed Victuallers). Some family history societies publish licensing records. You may also find websites covering pubs in your area. For example, the Norfolk Pubs website www.norfolkpubs.co.uk/ gives details of pubs in Norfolk, including:

◆ the name of the pub;
◆ the type of license (e.g. beerhouse);
◆ the address and the Hundred division in which it was situated;
◆ which brewery owned the pub;
◆ licensees with dates;
◆ if the pub is now closed, when it closed;
◆ photographs (in some cases);
◆ miscellaneous information (for example if it was a stopping point for coaches; details of sales particulars).

You also have a much better chance of finding information about the building and the landlord/landlady in the street directories. See Chapter 3 for further details about using street directories.

There's also likely to be information about the pub in local newspapers. There may be information about licensing – for example, if the license was refused the reasons are likely to be reported by the local press.

Another possible source of help is the Pub History Society: www.pub-historysociety.co.uk.

Former vicarages, churches and chapels

If your house was a former vicarage, rectory, church or chapel, you may find more information about the building among the parish records, which are likely to be deposited in the local record office. You may find a plan of the building, or information about the building in the glebe terriers, which will give at least a description of the property.

Former schools

If your house was a former school or a schoolmaster's cottage you may find more information about the building among the school records. These could include deeds, plans and log books. If the school has closed the records may be deposited in the local record office. If the school has moved the head teacher or local education authority may be able to help you with more information.

You may find details of the school in street directories. For example, White's *Norfolk Directory* (1845) refers to the National School in Attleborough, 'built in 1841, at the cost of £700, and attended by about 70 boys and 80 girls'. Smaller schools in larger towns or cities may have even more detail.

If you can pin down the date when the school was built or opened. or you know of any major events such as epidemics, royal visits, floods or fires, you may be able to find reports about them in the local newspapers.

Former hospitals

If your house was a former hospital you may find more information about the building among the hospital records. If the hospital has closed the records may be deposited in the local record office. If the hospital has moved the press office at the hospital may be able to point you in the right direction.

Again, you may find details of the hospitals in the street directories, including when it was built, how much the building cost, its funding including the names of any benefactors, how many patients and surgeons there were, and the officers of the charity – president, treasurer, physicians, surgeons, secretary, apothecary and matron.

As with schools, if you can pin down the date when the building was built, opened or extended, or you know of any major events such as epidemics, royal visits, floods or fires, you may be able to find reports about them in the local newspapers.

Former toll houses

If your house was a former toll house you may find more information about the building, such as details of leases, or plans, among the records of the turnpike trusts. Turnpike trusts had to produce annual accounts and enrol them in the Quarter Sessions. Both sets of records are kept in local record offices.

Former almshouses

If your house was a former almshouse you may find more information about the building among the reports of the charity commissioners, which are kept in local record offices.

Other institutions

If your house was built for an institution, for example a workhouse, you may find more information about the building among the institution's records. If the institution has closed the records may be deposited in the local record office. If it has moved to another building it's worth contacting the institution to see if they're able help you with more information.

Again, you may find details of a workhouse or institution and the name of its master or head in street directories. If it's in a major town you may find information such as:

- when it was built;
- what work the inmates did (for example, in St Andrew's Workhouse in Norwich it was the manufacture of worsted and cotton goods);
- how many people were accommodated;

- the expenditure of the workhouse;
- when the guardians are elected;
- names of the officers (master, apothecary, cashier, clerk, reliving officer, removal officer, schoolmaster/mistress) and possibly how much their annual salaries were.

Again, if you can pin down the date when it was built or opened, or you know of any major events such as epidemics, royal visits, floods, exhibitions or fires, you may be able to find reports about them in the local newspapers.

Mills

If your house was attached to a mill you may find more information about the building in specialist archives such as the Mills Archive www.millsarchive.com. There may also be local specialist archives or organisations that may be able to help you with more information.

Again, there may be information about the mill in local newspapers. However, unless it appears in an index made by a previous researcher, you may be in for a long search and you might not find the information you're looking for.

8

Who Lived There? Deeds and Taxation Records

This chapter deals with:

◆ the owners and occupiers of your house.

As well as personal records such as parish registers, census returns, and will and probate records, and references to owners/occupiers in street directories, there are other records that can help you trace the owners and occupiers. As always, it's best to work backwards and you may need to work with different sources to keep the trail going. You may also find that the sources also shed light on the building as well as on the occupiers and owners.

This chapter covers the different deeds and taxation records that can help you find out who lived in your house – what they are, where to find them and where to go next. These include:

◆ title deeds;
◆ Land Registry;
◆ manorial documents;
◆ taxation records – hearth, land, windows, poll;
◆ rate books.

The best place to start is with the deeds and land registry entries. If you don't have a complete set of deeds you should still be able to find out information about the occupants through other sources – such as census returns (1841–1901), rate books and taxation lists, electoral rolls and street directories.

Mill House was particularly intriguing for me because there was a legend about the house: that the miller had strangled his wife in a fit of jealous rage, thrown her body down the well, and then burned himself on a bread-oven and died from septicaemia. His ghost was supposed to haunt the house. Would there be any documentary evidence?

TITLE DEEDS

Before the Law of Property Act 1925 the only way to prove your good title to the land was to produce all the deeds. Every time the land changed hands a deed was written out and the 'abstract' (i.e. details such as the owner's name and the property involved) were written on the outside of the deed. Because previous owners might need to show that they'd bought the property from Mr A, who in turn had bought it from Mr B and so forth, deeds were often kept in 'bundles' so the legal rights could be traced back to the first transaction. Obviously, every time the property was sold the 'bundle' of deeds would grow bigger.

Your mortgage provider or solicitor should be able to let you see the deeds, though note that some mortgage providers may charge you to look at them.

Not all the deeds may be available. There are several reasons for this.

♦ Some deeds may be abstracts of title rather than the original deeds. If the owner of several properties sold off just one cottage, the original title deeds were still relevant to the rest of the estate, so wouldn't be given to the new owner. In these cases the solicitor's clerk would write out all the relevant abstracts of title for the new owner. An example of an abstract of title (for Mill House in Attleborough) is in Appendix 2.
♦ Some deeds may have been kept by previous owners.

◆ Some deeds may have been deposited in the local record office – note that they're often not indexed so you may need to search through a lot of documents in the 'minor collections' section of the archives.

Working with deeds

Deeds tend to contain a lot of legal terms, so you need to have some knowledge of property law – and note that they're often written in Latin until the sixteenth century. Deeds from the early twentieth century or before are likely to be handwritten rather than typewritten.

Earlier deeds are written on parchment, which feels slightly greasy to the touch. They will need very careful handling. They may be hard to unfold without damaging them, and if they haven't been opened for years you won't be able to open them completely flat. You're likely to see a 'title' written on the back – that is, on the outside of the folded document – which identifies what's contained in the document. For example, the conveyance for Mill House in 1912 has written on the outside:

Dated 18th October 1912
The Surviving Trustees of the Will of the late Mr Frederick Wright
to
Mr Charles Hy. Howard
Conveyance
of a Dwelling house, Stable, Paddock and premises situate all at Attleborough
in the County of Norfolk

The further back the deeds go, the harder you may find it to read the handwriting of the clerk. It's best to work backwards, so you get a feel for the format of the documents, which doesn't change that much over the years, and this means you won't have to spend quite so long deciphering words in earlier deeds. It's also worth making yourself an 'alphabet' of the script used, by using example letters from words you know as definite, to help you read the more difficult to decipher words.

Abbreviations

Because writing out every single word in full would be time-consuming and would also increase the amount of parchment needed and therefore the expense of producing the document, the solicitor's clerk tended to abbreviate words that were used frequently in deeds and titles of abstract. A big clue to an abbreviation is when there's a line written just above a word – this tells you that there are some letters missing.

Some of the more common English abbreviations, together with the full version and how the expanded abbreviation should be written in a transcription, are shown in Appendix 1.

Title deeds of property (freehold or leasehold)

Freehold property is when person A sells a property outright to person B. Between the sixteenth and nineteenth century there were two forms of conveyancing:

- **Bargain and sale**: where the owner of the property agrees to sell the property to the buyer at a set price.
- **Lease and release**: where the owner leases the property to another person for a year, and then the day after the end of the lease there is a 'release', so the lessor (the owner) gives up the right to recover the property from the lessee (the person who leases the property but wants to buy it). Once the release was made, it was effectively the same as an ordinary bargain and sale.

There are also leaseholds, where the owner of the property (landlord) rents the property to someone else (tenant). Most leases were for:

- a year;
- a term of years (usually seven years or a multiple of seven years);
- a term of lives (usually three).

Freehold conveyances will show the following.

- The date of the transaction, sometimes referred to as the 'date of execution' – it may be shown as a date in modern terms (e.g. 1 July 1790) or it might be shown as a regnal date (e.g. 1 July 30 George III – this is the 30th year of George III's reign, which is the period 25 October 1789 to 24 October 1790).
- The names of the seller and buyer, who may be referred to as the parties to the deed – first party, second party and so on.
- The consideration – price paid to purchase the property.
- A clause defining the type of conveyance – bargain and sale or lease and release, as described above.
- A description of the property – usually starts 'all that…'.
- Any 'covenants' or 'indemnities' – special conditions. For example, with Mill House the purchaser had to agree not to build in front of a certain line; and in the first house I bought, a nineteenth-century terraced house in the middle of Norwich, the covenant in the deeds stated that we were not allowed to keep pigs or dig up bricks.
- Witnesses, usually the parties to the deed and sometimes independent witnesses; each will make a seal and signature.

Leases will show the following.

- The date of the transaction.
- The names of the owner and lessee.
- A description of property, often along the lines of 'hath sett to farm' or 'hath to farm let'.
- The period of lease, often a year, multiple of seven years or a term of lives, usually three.
- The annual rent.
- Any 'reservations' to the landlord, such as rights to woods or minerals on the land – these were fairly common.
- Any 'covenants' – special conditions.

The deeds should give a short description of the property and its location. They will also give the names of former owners and occupiers. If there is an enfranchisement deed, this shows that the building once belonged to a manor (i.e. was copyhold) so there may be records of the building in the manor court rolls and books. Copyhold tenure was abolished in 1925.

From a series of title deeds you should be able to identify successive owners. The deeds may also name tenants, former owners and occupiers, and sometimes adjoining neighbours as well, which is useful when trying to identify property in early rate books.

Unfortunately, the description of the actual buildings is unlikely to be precise because the purpose of title deeds is to establish the legal rights in a property. The house may be described as a 'messuage' (the legal term for a dwelling house) in the parish of X, in the occupation of Mr A. Description of lands may be a little more precise, giving field names. There may be references to boundaries, giving the names of the people who owned or occupied adjoining properties. There may also be a plan of the property, although these tend to be rare before 1850.

In the case of Mill House the deeds for 1891 included a title of abstract which led back to 1850 and there were also indemnities. The conveyance of November 1892 showed a plan of the land and stated who owned the adjoining lands. The land belonging to Mill House was shaded, as can be seen in picture 8.1 below.

8.1 Plot of Mill House from conveyance of 1892, showing adjoining landowners' names.

If a right of way is shown (as on the plan in 8.1 above) the deeds tend to be quite informative because they need to be precise about the rights given.

You may also find other documents preserved with the deeds – these might include:

- probate copies of wills and inventories (see Chapter 9, page 154);
- sales particulars (see Chapter 7, page 99);
- mortgage details (see Appendix 2, page 178, for an example of mortgage details in the abstract of title);
- insurance policies.

LAND REGISTRY

The Land Registry was set up in 1862 to develop a register of titles to freehold and leasehold land, and about two-thirds of property titles in England and Wales are registered with the Land Registry. Since 1988 the public has been allowed to see the information held on the Land Register. For properties that have been registered the information includes:

- the location and extent of the property;
- the owner's name and address;
- if there are any mortgages on the land;
- if there are any rights of way on the land;
- the price paid (since April 2000).

You can also get a plan of the land, but the plan doesn't show the internal layout of the property.

You can view some of the information online, for a fee, at the Land Registry's website www.landregisteronline.gov.uk. You will need a copy of Acrobat Reader on your computer to be able to view the information, which is downloadable as a PDF (portable document format).

You can also trace the history of the owners through the Land Registry, which can provide copies of all transfers since the property was first registered with them. There is an administration fee for this plus a further fee for each transfer they copy for you. However, these transfers won't necessarily go back to when the house was built, as the records will only go back to when the land was first registered – which might be some considerable time later than the property was built.

MANORIAL DOCUMENTS

The manor was the basic unit of administration from medieval times. They varied in size; one manor could cover several parishes, or there might be more than one manor within a parish, each only covering a few acres. In Attleborough, for example, there were three manors: Mortimers cum membris, Chantecleers and Crowshall. The manor of Mortimers cum membris also held land in the nearby village of Old Buckenham.

Each manor had a lord. Tenants of the manor had to pay rent and service to the lord of the manor, and also had to obey the customs of the manor, which were laws such as trade regulations and the use of highways. The way that the land within the manor was passed to other people (succession) was governed by the manorial court, known as a 'court baron'.

Until about 1733 manorial documents were written in Latin, though you may find that some books are written in English. Note also that regnal years are often used, particularly for documents before about 1700.

Documents from manorial courts include the following:

- **Rentals** – these were lists of all the names of tenants who held land in the manor, a description of their land and how much rent they paid (which might be in cash, service or produce). Rentals tended to be produced mainly when the new lord of the manor took over, so were not produced as often as accounts.
- **Bailiffs' accounts** – these showed the income and expenditure of the manor during a year, which usually began at Michaelmas (29 September). It showed the 'charges' (money received by the steward – rents, sale of produce and levy of dines) and 'discharges' (money paid out for purchasing grain or livestock, repair of buildings and labour).
- **Custumals** – these were a survey of rents and services the tenants had to pay to the lord of the manor, and the rights and obligations of the lord of the manor.
- **Extents** – these were descriptions and valuations of the items on the manor – the usual order is the manor house and its grounds, then any mills, then demesne land (arable, meadow, pasture, woods) and then tenants' rents and services. As time passed and the lord of the manor leased the land out to tenants rather than working it himself, the extents tended to be replaced by the rentals.
- **Maps** – these tend to be produced after the sixteenth century, and show the boundaries of the land and possibly details of the adjoining lands.

Among the papers you may find other documents relating to the administration of the manor, typically correspondence.

The earliest manorial records consist of rolls, which are pieces of parchment stitched together to make a long roll, or books. Some date back to the sixteenth century or even earlier. You may also find that some of the information is in 'bundles' – the pieces of paper within a bundle are unlikely to be uniform in size, and they can vary from scraps of about 3 by 10 centimetres through to large pieces which have been folded down to fit neatly with the other papers in the bundles. With the bundles, a former clerk of the manor may have written a brief description of the contents on the outside of each piece of paper.

If your house was originally held by a manor (for example, there is an enfranchisement deed or any reference to copyhold tenure among the deeds), you may find the manorial records a useful source of information, as the rolls will record the transfer of copyhold land between people, either by inheritance or by sale.

Note, however, that many manorial records are written in Latin. There's also no central place where manorial records are stored. They can be scattered between local archives, the National Archives and private estates, although the Historic Manuscripts Commission holds a manorial register and you can search the National Archives website www.nationalarchives.gov.uk for manorial records.

From about 1650 the main function of manorial courts was to register transfers of property. There were four types of landholders.

- **Freehold** – freeholders had secure tenure and had no restrictions on their right to dispose of their lands.

- **Copyhold** – copyholders were customary tenants. They held a 'copy' of the entry in the manor court roll which recorded them as tenants (hence the name).
- **Leasehold** – leaseholders held land that was leased for a specified time (often 21 years).
- **Tenant at will** – exactly as it sounds; tenants at will held their land at the will of the lord of the manor. They were often the poorest tenants.

Entries in the manorial rolls contain:

- descriptions of the property;
- the names of the new and the previous tenant;
- the date when the previous tenant was 'admitted'.

New copyhold tenants were admitted either because they inherited the property or bought it after the seller 'surrendered' it to the lord of the manor. This procedure was recorded in the court roll, and often other relevant documents such as wills and previous tenants' details were recorded as well.

If your property was once copyhold it's worth checking with your local record office to see what kind of manorial records they hold and if there's any kind of indexing that will help you find either the property or its occupiers. Properties were often referred to by the name of the first owner, even many years after his death.

Typical entries in manorial rolls

Rentals are often split between freeholders and copyholders. The freehold list will have a heading along the lines of *Liberri redditus burgagiorum de* [place name] (i.e. Free rents of burgages of [place name]), while the copyhold list will begin *Tenentes per copiam* (i.e. tenants by copy).

The types of entry you're likely to find in rentals include:

- Rental made and renewed by the oath of [person name] on [date] –
  the Latin form is *Rentale factum et renovatum per sacrum* [person
  name, date].
- [Person name] son of [person name] holds a tenement formerly
  belonging to [person name] his [relationship – e.g. grandfather]
  paying [amount of rent] – the Latin form is [Person name] *filius*
  [person name] *tenet tenementum quondam* [person name] *sui* [rela-
  tionship – e.g. grandfather] *solvendo* [amount of rent].
- [Person name] holds freely a messuage with appurtenances and ren-
  ders annually [amount of rent] – the Latin form is [Person name]
  tenet libere messuagium cum pertinentiis et reddit per annum
  [amount of rent].

You may see a reference to 'various burgages' (*diversa burgagia*) or 'certain parcels of demesne lands' (*certas parcellas terrarum dominicalium*).

There may also be references to the right by which the person holds the
land (*habendum et tenendum*) – this could be:

- holds for the term of his life (*tenet ad terminum vite sue*);
- by hereditary right (*de iure hereditario*);
- by gift of (*de dono*);
- by right of [person name] his wife (*de iure* [person name] *uxoris sue*).

When it comes to a more detailed description of land, you may see references such as these:

- What the land contains, e.g. 'one tenement with a garden' (*unum tenementum cum gardino*) or 'a cottage with a garden' (*unum cotagium cum
  gardino*) or 'a messuage' (*unum messuagium* – this is a dwelling house).

- The amount of land, e.g. 'containing one rood' (*continens unam Rodam*) or 'three acres of arable land' (*tres acras terre arabilis*) or a 'a virgate' (*unam virgatum* – this is a variable measure, often 30 acres).
- Where it's situated, e.g. 'abutting to the north on a croft of [person's name]' (*borealiter abbuttans super croftum* [*person's name*]).

In the court rolls you may find the record of someone asking for admission as a tenant. The usual legal form is that someone came to the manorial court 'in his own person' and asked for admission 'in open court' (the phrase you're looking for will be along the lines of '[name] *in propria persona sua et in plena Curia petit admitti tenens permissis predictis cum pertinenetiis*').

The admission of a new tenant usually follows the surrender of the land, which is often in the form: to this court came [name] in person and in open court surrendered into the hands of the lord of the manor, according to the custom of the aforesaid manor. (*Ad hanc Curiam venit* [*name*] *in propria persona sua in plena Curia sursum reddidit in manus Domini Manerii predicti per virgam secundum consuetudinum Manerii predicti…*)

Tracing a house through manorial records

I knew from the enclosure map that the plot for Mill House had once belonged to the manor of Attleborough Mortimers cum membris. I was delighted to find that some of the manorial records, including a rental from 1641, were held at Norfolk Record Office. Even better, it was written in English rather than in Latin.

The rental (reference NRO MEA 2/2) started with a list of numbered plots of land from previous rolls (working backwards from the present) and then listed tenants roughly alphabetically with the corresponding plot numbers next to their names. Finding the mill meant searching through the numbered plots to find the right piece of land, then searching through the list of tenants and matching the plot number next to them.

The description of the land in the rental was very patchy. However there were three interesting entries which seemed to refer to the mill.

- Plot 245 – this was listed as a record from the roll dated '6 April 14 Caroli Regis' (i.e. 5 April 1638 – the fourteenth year of Charles I's reign). The plot was described as 'severall pieces in Myll Field' – and plot 245 was written next to a name that looked like 'Robert Slom' (questionable, however, as there's a mark after the 'm' which means there was some form of abbreviation – the handwriting is far from easy to read!) Information in the parish registers made me wonder if it was actually meant to read Robert Howes and was simply written in the wrong place, as the 'Sl' looked very like the way the letter H was written (and in Stuart handwriting, it's quite hard to distinguish between the letters m and w), but a chat with the duty archivist in the records office dashed my hopes. The name was probably Slome or Slomer or something similar, but nothing like it appears in the parish records so I was unable to trace it further.
- Plot 341–2 – this was listed as a record from the roll dated '18 Aug 21 Jacobi' (i.e. 18 August 1623 – the 21st year of James I's reign) which referred to the 'Mill Field' (342) and a 'cottage and yard' (341), with a rental of £2, 3s and 0d. (Obviously that wasn't the cottage that exists today, which wasn't built until the nineteenth century, but it may have been its precursor.)
- Plot 343 – listed in the same roll as plots 341–2, referring to a parcel of land 'in SW fild' [sic] of 'Thos Okling, Millwright' together with a mill.

Frustratingly, plots 341–3 didn't appear next to anyone's name in the tenants' list – and Thomas Okling's name didn't appear there either!

In another bundle of the manorial documents (reference NRO MEA 2/24) there was a draft agreement from 1789 between 'William Windham of Earsham in the County of Norfolk, the Lord of the Manor of Attleburgh Mortimers', George Turner and the several copyhold and freehold tenants of the manor, regarding the licence to build a windmill. Although it didn't refer to the mill in the centre of town, it did help me pin down the date when one of the other mills was built, because it referred to 'waste ground or common pasture' at Haverscroft. This was the mill known as Dodd's Mill – the other mill shown on Faden's map of 1797.

Another bundle (reference NRO MEA 2/13) held a draft of 99-year lease for the 'piece of land called Tanmoor Common' (i.e. the same place), and was dated 'the 29th year of George the 3rd' (i.e. 1789). This bundle also held a tantalising document dated 20 September 1659 referring to 'the highway which leadeth from Lord's Windmill to the…' – but the next word is missing as the paper was folded at that point and had simply worn away. There was also a draft letter from Mr Franklin to George Turner, dated 16 September 1788, which stated, 'you may say that I think another mill would probably be an advantage to the inhabitants of the parish'.

So although the manorial documents were unable to confirm who owned the mill in the centre of Attleborough, they did confirm that it was the only mill in town before 1788 – so any documents before that date referring to a mill would therefore refer to 'our' mill.

TAXATION RECORDS
Hearth tax
In 1662 there was a tax of two shillings for every fire, hearth or stove in households. It was payable in two instalments, at Michaelmas (29 September) and Lady Day (25 March). The tax was difficult to collect and was very unpopular; it was abolished after March 1689. There were exemptions:

- houses rented at less than £1 a year;
- houses containing less than £10 of goods;

- hospitals;
- almshouses;
- paupers (if they had a certificate of exemption signed by the parish priest and churchwarden).

The assessments for Michaelmas 1662 to Lady Day 1666 and for Michaelmas 1669 to Lady Day 1674 are in the National Archives, series E179. Other years are held in county record offices, either on microfilm or microfiche.

Between 1666 and 1669 the tax was collected by commissions (free-lance collectors, known as 'farmers') and few lists of taxpayers survive for that era.

The other difficulty in using these records to trace the history of your house (for example, matching number of hearths to the records, or confirming details of a householder's name) is that the number of hearths might be inaccurate and might change from one assessment to the next. Not every householder's name is documented because of widespread evasion.

The records show:

- names of chargeable and non-chargeable households, arranged by county and then by parish;
- the number of hearths in the house;
- how much they had to pay.

Sometimes the returns (the actual amounts paid) were listed separately; in some lists the returns are marked on the assessments.

Some local history groups have published taxation records. *Norfolk Genealogy volume XIV* includes the hearth tax returns for Michaelmas 1664. The tax listing for Attleborough is described as being on membrane 34, face, column 2, under the heading of 'Townes in Shropham hundred Attleburrough'. And there is indeed a listing for the mill: 'Thos Syer at the Mill, iij' – and this is immediately next door to 'Mr Green at the cocke, vij'. Mill House is a two-minute walk away from the Cock pub, on the same street. The next nearest mill would have been the one on Rivett's Lane, which didn't exist until after 1797, and the one on Haverscroft, present-day Dodd's Road, which I knew from the manorial records wasn't built until 1789. Together with other documents in the manorial records dating from 1623, it suggests that a mill existed on the site of Attleburgh Great Mill in 1664. Thos Syer is also listed eight places before the listing at the Cock with an assessment of 'ij' – presumably for his private house. So I was able to add him to my list of occupiers/owners, along with a definite date (see Appendix 4).

Norfolk Genealogy volume XX contains the hearth tax assessments for Lady Day 1666. Unfortunately, the entry under Attleborough is very short and only refers to 'a not of what monys I Recd'. For the whole of 'Attelburgh' there were 192 hearths and the collector took £9 and 12s. Unfortunately, as the amount is not split into individual receipts, it's not possible to trace the mill any further.

Land tax

Land tax was levied each year between 1692 and 1949, though the tax itself wasn't abolished until 1963. The Clerk of the Peace in each county kept the copies of the land tax assessments. The tax was based on 4 shillings in the £ and was levied on land with an annual value of more than £1 a year. Catholics had to pay double from 1692–1831.

From 1798 landowners could sign a contract with the Land Tax Commissioners to pay a lump sum or buy government stock in exchange for freeing them from liability.

The 1798 assessments are held in the National Archives, series IR23 and IR24. The remainder of the records are archived in county record offices in the records of the Clerk of the Peace, found in the Quarter Sessions; they may also be on microfiche. However, it's worth nothing that the microfiche records are 'negatives' (i.e. white writing on a black background) and can be very difficult to read. The assessments may not have survived for every year. Also, not every householder's name is documented after 1798 because some paid the lump sum to avoid future taxation.

Survival of records before 1780 tends to be very patchy.

The 1798 assessments show which landowner signed the contract to free them from liability and also list the contract number. Contracts made from 1905-1950 include plans of the property.

The tax assessment records records show:

◆ the name of the landowner;
◆ the name of the occupier;
◆ a very brief description of property (usually 'house' or 'house and land', but there may also be descriptions such as 'shop' or 'mill' – however, note that these descriptions may not exist there in lists before 1825);
◆ the amount of tax paid.

The records were handwritten, although printed forms were used from about 1800.

For Norfolk the tax returns are listed within the Hundred, and then by parish within the Hundred. For Shropham Hundred (which covers Attleborough) there are records for 1781–1832, with gaps.

I knew from the 1830 trade directory that John Mann occupied the land in 1830. The tax records show that he owned the land from 1825–1832 (although there were various occupants during that time – see Appendix 4).

Tracing the owner and occupier before then was trickier. In 1824 Jno. (which should be noted is usually an abbreviation for John, not Jonathan) Cooper was listed, which ties in with the Enclosure records from 1815. However, Cooper isn't listed in the tax returns of 1823 but Mann is. During 1819–1822 it's impossible to tell who the landowner was as the records only list the names of the landowners, not their holdings. 1811–18 lists Jno. Cooper (with various occupants); and 1800–1808 may be Jno. Knights (listed in the 1793 Directory as a baker). However, we also know that Stephen Nobbs Stevens intended to auction the mill and land in 1804, so that rather muddies the water! In the four remaining sets of records – 1781, 1784, 1796 and 1797 – the handwriting is very difficult to read; there appears to be no record of Knights, even though newspaper cuttings from 1781 and 1783 confirmed that Knights occupied the windmill in that period, and the trade directory of 1793–8 also lists Knights as a baker.

Poll taxes

Poll taxes were collected in 1377, 1379 and 1381, then again after restoration of the monarchy in 1660, 1667, 1678, 1689, 1691, 1694, and 1697. The charge was based on people's social rank, occupation or office. It varied between poll taxes.

- In 1377 it was 4d per person aged over 14.
- In 1379 it was 4d per person over 16.

- In 1381 it was a shilling per person over 15 (and this led to the Peasants' Revolt).
- For the seventeenth-century taxes, people over the age of 16 paid a shilling (if they weren't otherwise chargeable) and children under 16 paid 6d. Paupers were excluded.

The poll tax records show the names of people who paid the tax and how much they paid. Some may also list occupations and relationships between household members.

Poll tax lists for the fourteenth century plus those for 1660, 1667 and 1678 are held in the National Archives in series E179; later ones are in series E182. County record offices hold some poll tax lists.

Not everyone is documented, due to widespread evasion of the tax. It's worth noting that the fourteenth-century lists are in Latin.

The poll tax records for Attleborough haven't survived locally, so I was unable to trace the occupants of the mill.

Window tax

The window tax was collected from 1696 to 1851. There was a flat rate house tax for part of these years, plus an amount which varied with the rateable value of the house. There was also a tax on the number of windows, which again varied:

- 1696–1766, on houses with ten or more windows;
- 1766–1825, on houses with seven or more windows;
- 1825–1851, on houses with eight or more windows.

Windows of business premises were exempt in some years. The occupier rather than the owner had to pay the tax, but people who didn't have to pay poor rates were usually exempt. Many people blocked up windows so they didn't have to pay tax.

The records show:

- name and address of taxpayers;
- number of windows in the house;
- tax paid.

The returns are generally found in the county record offices. However, survival is patchy – it's unusual to find a complete set of records – and details aren't always accurate.

Unfortunately, the window tax records for Attleborough haven't survived. The house had 12 windows, so it would have been included in the taxation lists from 1804 onwards.

RATE BOOKS

Before 1834 property holders had to pay a 'poor rate', i.e. money to the parish which would help keep the poor. The overseers of the poor in each parish kept accounts of the rate paid in special rate books. During the 1800s the rate was collected by the Boards of Guardians. In 1925 collection of the rates became the responsibility of the district councils.

Your local record office should have records of poor rate assessments; although they were produced yearly, the local record office might not have the assessments for all years for all areas. The earliest ones will date from around the mid 1600s and the later ones could be as late as the mid 1900s.

The occupier's name and the sum assessed will be listed. There isn't necessarily a full description of the property in the earlier records, but the later ones will be listed by address and give the occupier's name, the owner's name, a description of the property and the estimated size of the property, as well as a note of the amount paid.

If the name in the tithe apportionment matches the name in the rate book and land tax return, it will help you work backwards in the records because the rental value will probably tally with the amount shown in the tithe, and the position of the entry in the book is likely to reflect the tax collector's route. If the rental value changes it may show that the property has been altered or extended.

The surviving poor rate for Attleborough dates from November/December 1814. The only mill mentioned with land belonged to Thomas Dodd. However, there is a reference to Joseph Cooper, who may have been related to the owner of the land for our mill, John Cooper.

9

Who Lived There? Personal Records

This chapter deals with:

◆ the owners and occupiers of your house.

As well as taxation records and references to owners/occupiers in title deeds, leases and manorial records, there are other records that can help you trace the owners and occupiers. As always, it's best to work backwards and you may need to work with different sources to find the lines; and you may find that the sources also shed light on the building as well as the occupiers and owners.

This chapter covers different sorts of records to help you find out who lived in your house – what they are, where to find them and where to go next. These include:

◆ census returns;
◆ parish registers (baptisms, deaths, marriages);
◆ street directories;
◆ electoral registers;
◆ wills and probate records;
◆ insurance records;
◆ records of bankruptcy;
◆ records of civil and criminal courts.

CENSUS RETURNS

Census returns are records of who occupied a property on a particular day. The census was taken every ten years and records are closed to the public for 100 years.

The census returns up to and including 1831 are simply a count by overseers of the numbers of people (male and female), houses and families in each parish or township. For the most part they do not include names; but some enumerators made lists of names which are available at county record offices. Some family history societies have also published transcriptions.

The census returns from 1841 onwards are more useful because they give more detail. The census takers tended to use the same route, so it's possible to follow the records backwards from 1901 by checking details of the neighbours. However, remember that properties were built and demolished over the years, so the reference number of the house you're trying to track down won't necessarily be the same in every census.

The originals of the 1841–91 census for England, Wales, the Channel Islands and the Isle of Man are kept in the Family Records Centre in London. However, the ones for your county should also be available in your local record office and in some local studies centres, either on microfilm or on microfiche. You can also search digital images and transcriptions of the 1901 census at www.1901censusonline.com. It's free to search the indexes although you'll pay a small fee to see the census pages and transcripts. You can also search the 1891 census at www.ancestry.co.uk, though again this is for a fee; it's worth asking your local library if they have a subscription to ancestry.co.uk, in which case you can access the site on a computer at the library without charge. The Society of Genealogists www.sog.org.uk also holds copies of the returns 1841–61 and 1891 on microfilm.

Census returns for Scotland are at the General Register Office for Scotland, though there is a computerised index to the 1881, 1891 and 1901 census at the Family Records Centre. You can also search the indexes online for a small fee at www.scotlandspeople.gov.uk/.

It's also possible to buy CD-roms which cover the census returns for one county in a particular year, from specialist genealogy suppliers. You can also buy microfiche copies of registration sub-districts from the National Archives.

Some difficulties with census returns

The census only lists the people who stayed at the house on census night. Places of birth are not always correct – the enumerator might have misheard them or spelled them wrongly. And people within the family may not be at home on census night: for example, servants who lived in at their place of work, people in the army and navy, or people in institutions such as workhouses, hospitals, schools and prison.

It's also possible that ages are inaccurate; some women didn't want to admit that they'd married a much younger man, and children are often shown as older than they really are because they could earn better wages as a 15-year-old say than as a 12-year-old. Family relationships could also be inaccurate; an unmarried woman's illegitimate child was often described as being the youngest child of her parents.

Census returns 1841

The details include:

- ◆ Name (only gives the first forename).
- ◆ Address (may be approximate, e.g. just the hamlet name, but may give the street name).
- ◆ Approximate age.
- ◆ Occupation.

◆ Whether the person was born in the same county as he/she was living in on the night of the census (if not, this may be S for Scotland, I for Ireland, F or FP for Foreign Parts, or NK for 'not known').

Full addresses are not always given and family relationships are not included. Ages of anyone over 15 were rounded down to the nearest five years (so if someone was 44 their age would be recorded as 40), and birthplaces only show if someone was born in that county, or if that person was born in Scotland, Ireland or 'Foreign Parts'.

The microfilm for the 1841 survey is a negative copy; it's quite hard to read white handwriting on a black background, particularly if the ink is feint.

Census returns 1851 onwards

The details include:

◆ Name.
◆ Address: streets, roads; it may also give house numbers and names. In 1891 this also included the number of rooms occupied by a family if less than five.
◆ Exact age at last birthday.
◆ Marital status: 'condition' – the usual abbreviations are 'mar' for married, 'u' for unmarried and 'w' for widow or widower.
◆ Rank, profession or occupation. Children are often noted as 'scholars'. In 1891 there are also columns for employer, employed or 'neither employer nor employed' – the latter means 'self-employed'. In 1901 it's 'employer, worker or own account' and there's also a column 'if working at home'.
◆ Relationship to the head of the house, e.g. wife, son, daughter, sister, brother, visitor.
◆ Parish and county of birth.
◆ Notes, i.e. if the person is deaf-and-dumb, blind, 'imbecile or idiot', or lunatic – by 1891 the last two categories are lumped together.

Census enumerator books

The front pages of the enumerator books describe the boundary of the enu-meration district. The number of people enumerated is a running number on the left-hand side of each page; the house number might appear in the second column next to the street name, or is otherwise unlisted.

The originals (and a microfilm set for the whole of England and Wales) are kept in the National Archives at the Family Records Centre. However, the ones for your county should also be available in your local record office on microfilm.

Tracing a house back through the census

I found it trickier than I'd expected to trace the details of Mill House through the census. There were six households listed in Mill Yard in 1901, and it wasn't immediately obvious which one was Mill House. The occupant of number '23' (i.e. the 23rd house enumerated in that section – the house didn't have a number) was 64-year-old widow Hannah Wright, and I knew from other sources that in 1901 the cottage was owned by Anna Wright, who'd inherited it from her husband Frederick. (It could be that the enumerator misheard or misspelled Anna as Hannah: the census entry for 1871 matches her name and age.) But number '24' was occupied by the Gathergoods – who I knew from other sources were tenants of Mill House by 1912. So I decided to note down the details of all the properties in Mill Yard, as well as one particular neighbour – number '30' on Levell Street was occupied by 57-year-old shopkeeper Charles Wright, whom I thought was likely to be Anna Wright's brother-in-law.

In 1891 the area was known as Mill Yard, off Levell Street – the street clearly wasn't known as Connaught Plain or High Street at that point. This time the house was possibly number '29' – with 45-year-old Emma Thompson as the head of the house, living with her younger aunts Alice Wright and Amelia Wright.

In 1881 the area was known as Mill Yard, off Levell Street. The head of the house at number '32' was Martha Wright, 70-year-old widow and cottage owner. I knew from the deeds that Martha had lived there in 1881 – so this was definitely the right house, and when I looked at the details of the neighbouring properties I could see that the neighbours had stayed the same over the years: some of the women's surnames had changed, but the age, birthplace, occupation and marital status details proved them to be the same people.

In 1871 the area was still known as Mill Yard. The head of the house at number '33' was Martha Wright – aged 60, deriving her income from houses. This tied in with the 1881 survey. With her lived her married son John Wright, a 28-year-old plumber and glazier, her unmarried son Ellis, a 20-year-old journeyman carpenter and her 17-year-old spinster daughter, Sarah, whose occupation was not given. The family lived nearby: at '36' Market Street, 38-year-old railway porter Frederick Wright (who I knew from the deeds bought the house in 1892) lived with his 34-year-old wife Anna and their children –William aged 11, Alfred aged 7, Anne aged 5 and Charles aged 3.

In 1861 the census return doesn't even mention Mill Yard. Number '34' Levell Street was occupied by 50-year-old widow Martha Wright, a 'proprietor of homes' (which ties in with her occupation in the 1871 survey), with her 15-year-old dressmaker daughter Martha, Ellis aged 10, Sarah aged 7 and a visitor, 13-year-old Emma E. Spraggs.

In 1851 Levell Street appears to be known as 'Meer Street'. Martha Wright (aged 40) is listed at '32' – along with John Wright (carpenter, aged 43), her children Frederick aged 19, Charles aged 17, Arthur aged 14, Alfred aged 10, John aged 8, Emma, aged 5 (interestingly Emma appears to be known as Martha by 1861), 2-day-old Eliza (probably a mis-transcription or mishearing of the name 'Ellis') and her sister-in-law Ann Wright, a 55-year-old-nurse who was presumably helping with the baby.

1841 was a much smaller survey – but it was also much harder to pin down the house. I knew the house existed then, from the newspaper advertisement (see Chapter 7). I also knew from the title deeds (see Appendix 2) that John and Martha Wright had bought the cottage in 1850 from Thomas Banks; and from the tithe survey (see page 89) and the land tax returns (see page 127) that the land was occupied by John Mann in 1845.

There was no sign of Thomas Banks or John Mann in the 1841 census, but the Yeomans family was listed in Queen Street. John Yeomans was a 40-year-old miller, living with his wife Hannah and his 20-year-old son Elizah (a misspelling of Elijah, according to the parish records), who was also a miller, and their youngest children Carter aged 13 and Mary aged 8. Next door to the Yeomans lived 30-year-old Martha Wright and her wheelwright husband John (also aged 30), with their children Frederick aged 9, Charles aged 7 and Alfred aged 10 months.

It was very tempting to assume that John Yeomans was a mistranscription of John Mann. John Mann is listed in the Attleborough land tax registers from 1823–32 (and where buildings are mentioned, he and Thomas Dodd are the only ones in the area listed as having a mill as well as a house and land). He was '40' in 1841 (in practice that means anything up to the age of 45), so he could well have owned the land when he was in his early twenties. But tracing him through the parish register made it clear that Yeomans probably wasn't the miller, though he may have worked at Attleburgh Great Mill.

There are other millers listed in Attleborough on the 1841 census: 80-year-old Thomas Avis on Norwich Road, 60-year-old Thomas Dodd and 42-year-old William Harris in Haverscroft, 30-year-old Samuel Wright at Besthorpe Lodge, and 35-year-old David Palmer and 45-year-old Robert Lovett at 'near Carr Street' in Besthorpe. None of these areas is near to the mill in Mill Yard.

Queen Street is probably modern-day Queen's Road, which leads out of the town to Ellingham Road. The Road Order map from 1814 (see picture 6.8 on page 94) doesn't show either the mill at Haverscroft (belonging to Thomas Dodd) or the mill in the town centre (or, for that matter, other buildings shown on Faden's map of 1797). Queen Street isn't named, and the stretch known as London Road, the High Street and Exchange Street is simply shown as Turnpike Road. But there are two named fields: Mill Field and Mill Piece. Mill Field equates to a plot just above Mill House, and a footpath (which was meant to be 'stopped up' in 1814) leads there from Queen Street. It's certainly possible that John Yeomans was the miller there – but it's also probable that John Mann (who also had a mill at Shropham) was the master miller and Yeomans was a journeyman miller (i.e. a man who was qualified but who didn't have any apprentices).

PARISH REGISTERS (BAPTISMS, DEATHS, MARRIAGES)

If you know a name of a previous owner or occupier from a title deed, you may be able to trace that person through parish registers to confirm details or add more information to your knowledge. This assumes that this person was born, married or died in the parish relating to the house, or had children while living in the house. The census records may be able to help you there if the 'place of birth' is filled in. If the dates don't tally with any of the census returns, then it's a matter of pot luck and searching through the church registers for that particular parish to see if you can spot the name. If you know that the person who lived in your house was born or married in another parish, you'll need to check the records of that parish.

Before the civil registration of births, marriages and deaths was centralised in England and Wales on 1 July 1837, records of baptisms, marriages and burials were made in the church or chapel where they took place. These records are known as parish registers and they record baptisms, marriages, burials and banns in the Church of England from 1538 onwards. However, not all registers have survived and those dating before 1598 are likely to be copies of earlier books.

From 1 July 1837 all births and deaths had to be reported to a local registrar, who reported them to the superintendent registrar in the district. The superintendent kept one copy and sent a separate copy every three months to the Registrar General. With weddings the church took two registers; one was kept by the church and the other was sent (once filled) to the superintendent registrar in the district. Every three months the church official also sent a copy of entries in the register for the last quarter to the Registrar General.

For marriages in church, banns were called for three Sundays before the wedding in the church where the bride and groom were to be married, and if one of them lived in another parish the banns would also be called in the church of that parish. If the couple married by licence the couple could marry on the same day as the licence was issued, or the day after. Licences were more expensive than banns. A special licence meant that the marriage could take place anywhere, but was rare because only the Archbishop of Canterbury or his officials could grant it. The common licence named one or two parishes where the marriage could take place, and could be issued by archbishops, bishops, archdeacons, ministers or officials entitled to act on their behalf (known as 'surrogates'). Licences were often accompanied by bonds, which were sworn statements by a couple's friends or relatives that:

- there was no impediment to the marriage;
- the couple would marry in a specified church;
- the bond money (i.e. how much money they would forfeit if the licence was not complied with).

What information they contain

Baptism registers before 1813

- date of baptism;
- child's name;
- parents' names (though sometimes only the father's name is given).

Some registers will include the father's occupation, the child's date of birth and the mother's maiden name.

Baptism registers 1813 onwards

Baptisms were entered into pre-printed standard registers. Columns were included for:

- date of baptism;
- child's name;
- parents' names;
- parish of residence;
- father's trade or occupation;
- the name of the officiating minister.

Sometimes the date of birth and mother's maiden name were included.

Marriage registers before 1754

- date of marriage;
- names of the bride and groom.

Sometimes the groom's occupation is listed.

Marriage registers 1754-1837

As with baptisms, marriages were entered into pre-printed standard registers. Between 1754 and 1837 all couples had to marry in an Anglican church for their marriage to be legally valid; only Quakers and Jews were exempt.

The information recorded includes:

- date of marriage;
- names of the bride and groom;
- parish of residence for both bride and groom;
- whether the marriage was by banns or licence;
- whether the groom was a bachelor or a widower;
- whether the bride was a spinster or a widow;
- signatures of bride and groom, the officiating minister and two witnesses (those unable to write would make a mark).

There may be additional information, such as the groom's occupation or the name of the bride's father.

Banns registers after 1754
The registers of the banns were kept from 1754. Before 1823 you should find them in the back of the marriage registers; after 1823 they were kept in separate registers.

The information in the banns includes:

- names of the bride and groom;
- the three dates when the banns were read out in church.

They may also record the bride's and groom's places of residence, and if one of the spouses lived in another parish the banns register would also note that parish.

Marriage registers after 1837
Births, marriages and deaths were registered centrally from 1 July 1837. Church marriage registers took on the same format as civil marriage certificates. The information includes:

- marriage date;
- names of the bride and groom;
- parish of residence for both bride and groom;
- occupation (usually the groom and sometimes the bride);
- ages ('of full age' usually means 21 years or over);
- whether the groom was a bachelor or a widower;
- whether the bride was a spinster or a widow;
- name and occupation of the father of both bride and groom;
- whether the marriage took place by banns or licence;
- signatures of bride and groom, the officiating minister and two witnesses (those unable to write would make a mark).

Burial registers before 1812

- date of burial;
- name of person buried (family relationships may be given, e.g. wife of, widow of, son/daughter of – this tends to be mainly in the case of women and children).

Sometimes the age at death and occupation was included. It may also be recorded if the person was from the workhouse ('pauper'). Some clerics give more information than others, e.g. if someone had been murdered the cleric might have recorded some of the details and whether the murderer was caught and paid the penalty (as with, for example, the entry for Samuel Alden at Attleborough in 1807 mentions his 'horrid murder' and the fact that his wife Martha 'paid the price on Castle Hill').

Burial registers after 1812

As with births and marriages, burials were entered into pre-printed standard registers. Columns were included for:

- date of burial;
- deceased's name;

- parish of residence;
- age at death;
- officiating clergy.

Clergymen sometimes added a family relationship, e.g. wife of, widow of, son/ daughter of; this tends to be mainly in the case of women and children. Occasionally the cause of death is listed – sometimes as 'p' or 'pest' if it was the plague.

Where to find them
- County Record Offices.
- Family Records Centre (part of the National Archives) at 1 Myddleton Street, London EC1R 1UW – for union indexes of births, marriages and deaths registered officially in England and Wales from 1 July 1837 up to about 12 months ago. They are known as 'union' indexes because registration districts took their name from the poor law union in which they were based. You can search the indexes online for a small fee at www.1837online.com – note that you will need to register, give a password and download a special viewer so you can use the indexes.
- Scottish General Register Office – for indexes of Scottish registers of births, marriages and deaths since 1 January 1855, and of births and marriages in the Church of Scotland from about 1553. There is also a computerised link to these records at the Family Records Centre, or you can search online at www.scotlandspeople.gov.uk and view indexes of birth registrations 1855–1903, marriages 1855–1928 and deaths 1855–1953, again for a small fee.
- Family History Societies may also have copies of the indexes.

Potential difficulties
Under the Calendar Act 1752 the first day of the year moved from Lady Day (25 March) to 1 January. Before then January 1–March 24 was the last quarter of a year. So you need to add a year to convert dates in

records to 'modern' times. For example, the record may show a date of 1 February 1605 (also known as 'old style'), but it's what we would know as 1 February 1606 ('new style'). It's best to write it as 1 February 1605/6 – this avoids ambiguity because then anyone reading your research will know that 1605 was written in the document, but 1606 is the 'real' year in the modern calendar.

Also, before the nineteenth century there were no rules about how entries should be set out in the registers or what details should be included, so they're not consistent between parishes or even between different clerics in the same parish. There are also likely to be gaps during the period of the Civil War, 1645–60.

Usually entries are chronological. However, the layout varies – early registers tend to mix baptisms, marriages and burials, whereas later ones have baptisms at the front, marriages in the middle and burials at the back. Because parchment and paper were expensive, the clergy used all the space in the registers – so sometimes when the last page had been filled they squeezed entries into little gaps found earlier on in the registers.

Some parish register entries are in Latin, particularly those before the eighteenth century. Some of the most common phrases used are:

- *baptisatus / baptisata est / erat / fuit* – was baptised;
- *natus/nata* – was born;
- *filia* – daughter;
- *filius* – son;
- *gemini* – twins;
- *conjuncti fuerant* – were joined in marriage;
- *copulati sunt/erant* – were married;
- *nupti erant* – were married;
- *nupsit* – married;

- *licentiam* – by licence;
- *bannum* – by banns;
- *uxorem duxit* – he took to wife (i.e. married);
- *sepultus / sepulta* – buried;
- *mortus* – died;
- *eodem die* – on the same day (as the previous entry);
- *ultimo die mensis* – on the last day of the month of;
- *primo die mensis* – on the first day of the month of;
- *parochia* – parish;
- *in comitatu/in agro* – in the county of;
- *ibidem* – in the same place;
- *extraneus* – a stranger.

Deaths tend to be registered because after 1837 you could only bury someone if you gave the church a death certificate or coroner's certificate. However not all births between 1837 and 1874 were registered because you didn't have to inform the registrar of a birth, and many people thought that a baptism was a legal alternative to registration. The 1874 Births and Deaths Act meant that you could be fined if you registered a birth more than 42 days after the event, or didn't register it at all: so birth dates might not be accurate because if parents were late in registering a birth they'd tell the registrar a different date in order to avoid a fine!

There's also the fact that you only had to live in a parish for three weeks before the cleric could describe you as 'otp' or 'of this parish'.

There are a lot of gaps in registers during the English Civil War and Commonwealth periods, because some priests had to leave their parishes for political reasons. From 1653–60 the Parish Register was responsible for the registers rather than the church; this was a person elected by the ratepayers who had been approved by local magistrates. Births rather than baptisms were recorded, and deaths rather than burials. Also from 1653–60, only marriages conducted by the local JP were legal, and notices of 'publication of intention to marry' were posted in the market place for three weeks before the wedding rather than having banns called.

Note that if you're using a microfilm or microfiche copy of records, it will be a negative copy (white text on a black background) and this can be hard to read for a long stretch of time.

Transcriptions

Some parish records have been transcribed and published (with indexes) by local genealogical societies; your local library should be able to tell you if something has been done in your area. Local history societies also publish transcriptions of some records on the web, so it's also worth checking via GENUKI.

Obviously this isn't a substitute for looking at the real thing. Handwriting can be very difficult to read, transcribers or typesetters can make errors or omissions, and indexers might not have noted something that you'd consider significant. It's also possible that with your knowledge from other records you can fill in some gaps. However, transcriptions are a quick way of pinpointing dates and leads to follow up in the original records.

Transcriptions of records for some areas are also available on CD-rom from the Parish Register Transcription Society www.prtsoc.org.uk.

Case study: finding a house's occupants via parish records

The parish registers of Attleborough (1552–1840) had been transcribed, edited and indexed by Sanderson and Palgrave-Moore and published by the Norfolk and Norwich Genealogical Society. I knew some of the names of occupants (see Appendix 4) and I also knew that a father's or bridegroom's occupation was sometimes listed in the parish records. I had high hopes of being able to corroborate information and maybe find new leads in the parish records.

I knew from indexes of wills that Robert Sparke, miller of Attleborough, died around 1559, and John Sparke, miller of Attleborough, died around 1566. The parish records confirmed that Robert was buried on 4 April 1559 and John was buried on 19 September 1566.

Reading the wills themselves shed a little more light on matters. Robert's will states: 'I bequethe to Elizabeth my wife my wind myll' – but adds that after her death it will go to 'my son Richard'. (Other parts of the will make it clear that Richard was younger than 21.) John's will states: 'I bequeath unto Valentyne Sparke my sonne my windemill in Attylburgh with all the furniture belongynge unto the same', so clearly at some point Elizabeth had sold the mill to John. The entries in the parish register only give the names and date of burial for both Robert and John, but it's likely they were brothers rather than father and son and that John was the younger of the two.

There was a record of the baptism of John, son of John Sparke, on 30 June 1566 (so clearly John lived just long enough to see his son's birth), and then Thomas, son of John Sparke (the younger) was baptised on 18 August 1583. However, John appears to be very young when his son was born – a minor, in fact, and he would have needed his parents' permission to marry. Interestingly, there's a record of the marriage of John Sparke to Margaret Carman on 13 April 1589 – but unfortunately the records don't give information about their marital status (i.e. spinster and bachelor, or widow or widower). So it's possible that Thomas's father John was a different John Sparke.

John Forbie, who became the rector of St Mary's in Attleborough in 1614, gave a lot of details in the burials register – often including biographical notes, such as the widow Ann Meakes who was '5 score and 14 years of age' when she died, but 'was rather to be more 120 years of age'; George Hanford 'a good smith but a bad husband'; and John Spoorele, who 'had overheated his bodie & so was inwardly moulten & his bloode thereby turned into a fatt watterie Couller'.

In Forbie's burial records, I found a completely unexpected entry giving a little piece of history from the mill: 'Thomas, son of Ralf Moore of Pulham, being slayne by the breaking of the [vane] of the Wyndmill in a great wynd' was buried on 4 January 1616/7.

The next mention of a miller is 1 December 1630, noting simply the burial of 'the child of Thomas Howes, myller'. There are records of baptism of three of Thomas's children: Robert, who was baptised on 6 February 1627/8, Roose (clearly a mis-spelling of Rose), baptised on 15 October 1629, and Elizabeth, baptised 18 February 1629/30. Given the dates, however, it's possible that the child buried in 1630 died at or shortly after birth, before he or she could be baptised.

Thomas himself appears to have been buried on 19 November 1661, on the same day as his grandson ('Thomas, son of Thomas Howes Junior').

Thomas Syer, who we know from the hearth tax listing was the miller in 1664, clearly wasn't married in the parish of Attleborough. He also didn't have children baptised in the parish and wasn't buried there either, as he isn't listed in the parish records.

The next miller we know of from other sources is John Knights in 1781. There are several baptism entries listing John Knights as the father of the child (though, as the rector didn't bother including the father's occupation in the entries, we can't be completely sure that he's our John Knights). The records hint that he married twice; the baptism register lists his children as:

- Mary, daughter of John Knights and Eliza[beth], 24 January 1763;
- Honoria, daughter of John Knights and Eliza[beth], 10 September 1764;
- Charles, son of John Knights and Eliza[beth], 22 June 1766;
- Mary, daughter of John Knights and Mary, 20 April 1772;
- Elizabeth, daughter of John Knights and Mary, 8 July 1773;
- Joseph, son of John Knights and Mary, 28 July 1774.

From 1813 until 1841 the father's occupation is included in the baptism registers, which helped me pinpoint a few millers:

- William Littleproud (daughter Ann baptised 1 January 1813; son William baptised 10 March 1815; daughter Alice Lindo baptised 20 December 1816; son John baptised 16 January 1819; son James baptised 18 August 1827).
- Thomas Dodd (son Henry James baptised 27 July 1814; daughter Eliza baptised 30 October 1818; son Thomas baptised 22 September 1822; son Frederick baptised 12 November 1823).
- Edward Sharman (son Thomas baptised 23 November 1817).
- John Rose (son Thomas baptised 22 May 1821).
- Robert Lock (daughter Mary baptised 12 February 1826).
- John Yeomans (son Carter baptised 31 March 1828; daughter Mary baptised 30 May 1833).
- James Ringwood (son Robert baptised 13 December 1831).
- Edmund Nurse (daughter Deborah Martha baptised 28 February 1832).
- Thomas Burroughs (daughter Caroline baptised 11 November 1832).
- William Warns (daughter Louisa baptised 10 December 1832).

Because the census records 1801–31 are just a headcount, we can't compare the census information with the parish records to place any of the millers. We know from other sources and the 1841 census that Thomas Dodd was based at the mill in Haverscroft; and we know from the 1841 census that John Yeomans lived next door to the Wright family (who owned Mill House from 1850).

From the census records alone it's tempting to speculate that Yeomans is the same person as Mann. The parish records shed a different light on matters: there is no record of John Mann (who also had a business at Shropham, so it's likely his details are in the Shropham parish registers), but an entry in the Attleborough baptism register shows that John Yeomans, son of Jonathan Yeomans and Elisabeth, was baptised as an infant on 3 June 1797. This would make him 44 on the night of the 1841 census – so he's likely to be the John Yeomans 'aged 40' in Queen Street. The marriage registers show that he married Hannah Upcraft on 16 February 1819 (preceded by banns; the witnesses were 'Sar. Lake and H. Johnson'). Their youngest children are shown in the list above, but they had three older children too: Elijah was baptised on 20 August 1820, James was baptised on 25 October 1823 (and buried three years later on 15 October 1826) and John was baptised on 22 August 1825. John Yeomans' occupation was listed as 'lab' (i.e. labourer) for the records of his first three children, so it's therefore very unlikely that he owned the mill or the land, although he may have worked there.

INTERNATIONAL GENEALOGICAL INDEX

The Church of Jesus Christ of Latter-day Saints is working on an ongoing project to build an International Genealogical Index (IGI) by extracting birth, baptism and marriage entries from records worldwide. It's useful if you're trying to trace someone who moved around a lot or you're trying to work out which one of several indexed registrations is the one you're looking for.

What information they contain

The first six columns are the ones you can use to locate parish records.

- Column 1: surname and first name.
- Column 2: name of parents or spouse.
- Column 3: gender (M = male; F = female; H = husband; W = wife).
- Column 4: event (A = adult christening; B = birth; C = christening; D = death or burial; F = birth or christening of first known child, in lieu of marriage date; M = marriage; N = census; S = miscellaneous; W = will or probate).
- Column 5: date of event.
- Column 6: place (town or parish).

Where to find them

Family History Centres from the Church of Jesus Christ of Latter-day Saints allow the the public to see the registers, though a small fee may be payable.

The IGI is also available at the Family Record Centre in London for the whole country (on microfiche) and online at www.familysearch.org.

County record offices or local studies centres may have microfiches for your county, neighbouring counties or even the whole of England and Wales; the library of the Society of Genealogists also has copies.

Potential difficulties

There may be transcription errors. The IGI doesn't contain every single parish register entry before 1837, and not all records are complete. And note that the IGI is copyright – if you wish to publish any of the information in print or on a website, you need to obtain permission.

STREET DIRECTORIES

Street directories are covered in more detail in Chapter 3. As well as using directories to trace the history of a building, you can use them to corroborate details from the census returns for the occupations – particularly after 1841 when occupations are listed on the census returns. They're probably more useful for larger urban centres, but you should still find a list of private residents and tradesmen in villages or towns. Obviously this doesn't cover the complete population of an area (servants and labourers are rarely included), but if the person who lived in your house was a tradesperson or seen as part of the local clergy and gentry, they may well be listed.

One problem with villages and smaller towns is that the street address or house often isn't given before the 1890s: this is probably on the basis that the population was still so small that anyone could tell you where (using our mill as an example) John Mann the miller lived.

See Appendix 3 for a list of the millers in Attleborough, which was helpful in pinning down who worked where and finding out who had been involved with Attleburgh Great Mill.

ELECTORAL REGISTERS

Electoral registers (sometimes called the Electoral Roll) record the names of people who are entitled to vote. They are arranged in order of electoral division, polling district and then alphabetically by voter or street. The series of registers starts in 1832, when they had to be deposited with the Clerk of the Peace. They contain the names of people who were eligible to vote (though house numbers and names are not always noted) and collections of the registers are held in local studies libraries and county record offices. Some will be original; others will be on microfilm or microfiche. Other archive sources that have copies include the British Library; the National Archives; and the Society of Genealogists.

Not all registers survive. Because they were large and took up a lot of storage space they were often thrown away when they were no longer current.

Earlier registers will be smaller because fewer people were entitled to vote. It's worth noting the dates of enfranchisement.

- From 1832: in the boroughs all male householders (i.e. including tenants) of land worth at least £10 a year, and in the counties owners of property worth at least £10.
- From 1867: in the boroughs all owners of dwelling houses and occupiers who paid more than £10 in rent a year, and in the counties all male householders of property worth £5 or who occupied land and paid rent of more than £50 a year.
- From 1884: all owners of dwelling houses and occupiers who paid more than £10 in rent a year (so this is most men over 21).
- From 1918: all men over the age of 21; all women aged over 30 who were householders or wives of householders.
- From 1928: all women over the age of 21.

It's also worth remembering that not everyone registers to vote, so electoral registers will never be complete: just because someone isn't listed, it doesn't mean they didn't exist, because they might not have registered to vote.

There are also poll books, which are published records of how people voted (before 1872, when the secret ballot was introduced). They are arranged by parish; poll books for towns often give the person's occupation.

Again, not all poll books for an area will be available, but it's worth checking the available ones against the records you have.

The poll books didn't shed any light for me on the owners of the mill in Attleborough.

WILLS AND PROBATE RECORDS

Wills are the documents by which people dispose of their property after their death. From the early 1500s to around 1750 an inventory (known as a probate inventory) of the deceased person's estate was filed with the will. The probate inventory was needed to assess the charges of the probate court.

Until 12 January 1858 probate (the proving of a will) was handled by the church courts; after that date they were transferred to a civil court. There is a printed calendar compiled for England and Wales annually listing all proved wills, i.e. those made legally valid.

The Statute of Wills 1540 meant that males over the age of 14 and females over the age of 12 could make a will; after 1837 they had to be aged 21 to make a will. Wills couldn't be made by lunatics, prisoners, traitors, heretics or slaves. Married women couldn't own property until the Married Women's Property Act 1882, so they could only make a will if their husband consented.

If someone did not leave a valid will, there may be an administration grant. This may tell you who had the grant to administer the estate, but probably won't tell you much else. The administration act or grant is also likely to be in Latin. (For example, research in the record office indices showed that there was a grant of administration for the Attleborough miller Thomas Syer in 1668 – but all the grant told me was that Thomas died intestate and the administrator was Gulielmo Syer, i.e. William Syer.)

The format of a will tends to include the following.

- A statement that this is the last will and testament of [person's name] of [address] in the parish of [parish name] – sometimes the occupation is included; there is usually some information about being of sound mind, and some religious wording (for example, in the will of Robert Sparke, he says 'first and formost [sic] I commend my soule into the hands of Almyghty God my maker and redeemer' and requests his body 'to be buryed in the church yard of Attylburgh').

- The appointment of executors (named, sometimes with addresses, occupations and relationship to the deceased).
- A statement of how debts and funeral expenses should be paid.
- A statement of how the estate will be distributed – the spouse is listed first, then children, then others. There may be specific bequests and information about how the property would be divided up if one of the beneficiaries dies before the person who made the will.

Administrations contain the name of the person appointed to administer the estate (usually a widow, child or brother, though sometimes a creditor), and the date will give you an approximate idea of the date of death.

The indexes to wills and administrations give the dates (and sometimes places) of death of the named people.

Calendars of wills list:

- the deceased's name;
- the date of death;
- where and when the will was proved (or administration was granted);
- the name of the executor (or administrator);
- the value of the estate (usually the figure before payment of debts or funeral expenses; and it may be listed as 'effects under £50').

The calendar may give the occupation of the deceased, executor or administrator, and in the second half of the nineteenth century it may also list the addresses of the executor or administrator and any relationship to the deceased.

Probate inventories list and value household furnishings and other goods that belonged to the deceased (except for land and buildings), often room by room. They would also list farm animals and equipment, items used for trade, the contents of shops, clothing, debts owed and debts due. In 1529 an Act of Parliament meant that if the deceased's possessions were worth £5 or more an inventory had to be made for the church authorities. Earlier inventories tend to be more detailed than later ones.

The printed calendars of proved wills are on microfiches in county record offices; they are also available at the Family Records Centre in London and the Probate Search Room. Copies of proved wills before 1858 may be available in your local record office; for example, Norfolk Record Office holds wills and administrations proved from the 1370s to 1858 on microfilm. Inventories would be held with the wills, usually among the church court records in county record offices.

Copies of wills and administration granted by civil probate registries in England and Wales since 1858 are held in the Public Searchroom, Principal Registry of the Family Division, 1st Avenue House, 42-49 High Holborn, London WC1V 6NP. You can try contacting your local probate office to see copies of wills and administrations from 1858 to the present, and your local record office or local studies department may have microfilm copies of the indexes to wills and administrations in England and Wales from 1858.

If you're looking for a will or administration grant between 1796 and 1903 you can start with the yearly indexes in the Family Records Centre (series IR 27), or with the registers which record death duty payments (series IR 26). The registers show when and where a will or administration grant was made. Scottish death duty registers from 1804 are in the National Archives of Scotland (reference IRS 5–14).

Some pre-1858 wills (particularly those of wealthy people) were proved by the Prerogative Court of Canterbury (PCC). These wills, together with administrations granted by this court, are held by The National Archives and can be seen on microfilm at the Family Records Centre (National Archives) in London. You can search indexes online from the 1300s to 1858 at www.nationalarchives.gov.uk/documentsonline although there is a small fee to view the digital images of the wills.

Death duties

There are three sets of records known collectively as death duties:

- legacy duty – this was payable between 1796 and 1949;
- succession duty – this was payable between 1853 and 1949;
- estate duty – this was payable between 1894 and 1975, when it was replaced by Capital Transfer Tax.

The records of the legacy duties 1796–1903 are held in the National Archives. However, from 1904 separate files, based on individuals, were kept by the Inland Revenue and destroyed 30 years after the files were closed.

The registers for the legacy duty on wills proved in county courts can be searched online at the National Archives' website www.nation-alarchives.gov.uk/catalogue/search.asp for a small fee.

You may find some succession records in local archives. I found two succession duty records relating to Frederick Wright (owner of the cottage in 1892), for property inherited from his uncle George. The format is usually:

- Register [letter] of the year [year] folio [folio number].
- An account of the Succession in Real Property of [inheritor name] [county name] [occupation] upon the death of [name of the deceased]

who died on [date] the Predecessor under the last Will and Testament of the said [name of the deceased] late of [town name] aforesaid dated [date of will] and proved on [date will proved] in the District Registry of [city name] of Her Majesty's Court of Probate & delivered by [inheritor name] of [town] his successor.

◆ Property details – including 'gross rack rental or annual value', saleable value, whether it's freehold or copyhold, tenant names, tenancy terms [e.g. 'from year to year'].

Succession duty registers may be of some use in helping you to track down relevant wills. Unfortunately, the records above related to other property than Mill House, so they weren't worth following up.

Some difficulties with wills and probate records

Fewer than one in ten people made wills or had them formally approved, and death duty registers only record estates that are liable to tax (i.e. were worth over a certain amount). It's also worth noting that probate grants or letters of administration were often dated several months after the date of death, and until 1898 the value of the estate in the calendars is for personal effects only, not real estate.

INSURANCE RECORDS

If you have an original fire mark plaque on your house the reference number will help you trace the policy entry in the company's records. For the most part the records to the major insurance companies' records aren't indexed, so it would be very difficult to trace a former policy. Local record offices may have partial indexes for local companies, and there is also an unpublished index for the Sun Fire Insurance Company, for 1710–31, in the Guildhall Library in London.

BANKRUPTCY RECORDS

If you know that someone who lived in your house was declared bankrupt you may be able to find more information in the bankruptcy records.

Until 1841 you could only be declared bankrupt if you were a trader (i.e. someone who earned their money by buying and selling things – by the late eighteenth century this included craftsmen) and owed more than £100; in 1842 this figure was reduced to £50. If you didn't qualify as a bankrupt you were termed an 'insolvent debtor' and could be put in prison indefinitely. From 1861 insolvent debtors could apply to be made bankrupt.

Bankruptcy notices appear in the *London Gazette*, *The Times* and in local newspapers.

The bankruptcy records are held in the National Archives for London cases. Records for cases 1842–69 will be held in local record offices among the records of bankruptcy courts, and records from 1869 will be with the records of county courts in local record offices.

There are Registers of Petitions for Bankruptcy for 1870–83 in the National Archives in series B 6/184-897, listed alphabetically by the bankrupt's surname.

Frustratingly, even though I knew John Knights had been made bankrupt in 1783, I was unable to trace the information any further than the notice in the local paper.

COURT RECORDS
Civil
If you know that someone who lived in your house was involved in a lawsuit you may be able to find more information in the civil records of the court.

Although the common law courts were held in Westminster, trials in civil disputes were usually held locally by the circuit judges. Records of quarter sessions, petty sessions and county courts are usually held in the local record office.

Criminal

If you know that someone who lived in your house was involved with a crime you may be able to find more information in the criminal records of the court.

Criminal trials took place at the assizes twice a year from the thirteenth century until 1971, when they were replaced by the crown courts.

Assize court records are held at the National Archives. They tend to be written in Latin before 1733 and don't give much detail about the accused. Just to muddy the waters a bit, the names given may be aliases and the occupation and address of the accused may also be suspect.

To find the case you want to look at, you need to know:

◆ the name of the accused;
◆ the county or circuit where the trial took place;
◆ the date of the trial.

Survival of assize records is patchy because when the files got too large, the assize clerk simply destroyed them. However, you may find printed calendars of prisoners and their offences in your local record office.

Assizes in London and Middlesex were held before the Lord Mayor before 1834, and from then in the Central Criminal Court. Some of the records are held in the National Archives and many can be accessed online at www.OldBaileyOnline.org.

There are criminal registers for England and Wales 1805–92 (held in the National Archives in series HO 27) which give details of the place of trial, verdict and sentence. There are also calendars of prisoners tried at assizes and quarter sessions from 1868 (held in the National Archives in series HO 140, but note that these records may be closed for 75–100 years).

Transcripts of assize proceedings don't tend to survive, but local newspapers, especially in the nineteenth century, often reported cases verbatim. (See Chapter 10 for more details about newspapers.)

Some Latin abbreviations continued to be used after 1733, including:

- ca null – *catalla nulla*, no goods to forfeit;
- cog ind – *cognovit indictamentum*, confessed to the indictment;
- cul – *culpabilis*, guilty;
- ign – *ignoramus*, we do not know (no case to answer);
- non cul nec re – *non culpabilis nec retraxit*, not guilty and did not flee;
- po se – *ponit se super patriam*, pleads not guilty and opts for jury trial;
- sus – *suspendatur*, let him be hanged.

There may also be prison records held at the local record office, which may include calendars of prisoners, gaol books and minutes.

Given the legend of the mad miller who murdered his wife, I hoped to find some kind of evidence in the records. However, the only record I could find of a murder in Attleborough was that of Samuel Alden by his wife Martha in 1806 – and Samuel had absolutely nothing to do with the mill. It's possible that one of the millers before the nineteenth century was the murderer, but I couldn't find any documentary evidence. There are various printed calendars of prisoners for Norfolk from 1693 onwards, but I could find no mention of anyone from Attleborough in the records between 1693 and the murder of 1806.

10

Other Sources

This chapter covers other sources of information including:

- local newspapers
- local historians
- and oral history.

NEWSPAPERS

There are two main types of newspapers: national and local. Unless an event of national importance happened at your house (or a previous owner/occupier was involved), you're more likely to find information in local newspapers rather than national ones. However, it's still worth running a broad-brush search through *The Times* online www.galegroup. com/Times to see if an event or a person made national news. If you live in a small village it's also worth running a search on the village name. If you find a mention in *The Times* it's likely that your local newspaper will have a more detailed report somewhere in the period between the week prior to *The Times*' report and the week after.

Working with local newspapers

The oldest provincial newspapers date from the early eighteenth century. They tend to be a single folded sheet with two columns per page, produced every Saturday, sometimes twice a week, on Saturdays and Wednesdays. Gradually, as print became cheaper and stamp duty on newspapers was repealed, newspapers grew larger (with around seven columns per page), contained more pages and were published much more frequently.

The earliest local newspapers contain a mixture of local news and advertisements, plus national and international news reprinted from London papers.

Advertisements can be a rich source of information, particularly if your house was owned by a tradesman or was a former shop or pub – but it does mean spending a lot of time combing through the archives, unless your particular local newspapers have been indexed by academics or library staff and the advertisements are included in the index.

Antiquarians occasionally produce 'annals' – a kind of digest of newspapers, which can help you to pinpoint the date of an event and then look up more detailed information in the newspaper itself. For example, in Norwich Charles Mackie produced two volumes of annals, based on the reports of the *Norfolk Chronicle and Norwich Gazette*. The index to the annals lists people who died and also events such as fires, floods, accidents, elections, murders, escapes from prison and the like. However, the annals usually have a bias towards the compiler's interests (in the case of Mackie, election and political coverage is particularly detailed) so even if you don't find something in a set of annals, there may still be a reference in the newspapers.

Where to find local newspapers

Previous copies of local newspapers tend to be available on microfilm nowadays to preserve the originals. They are usually found at the main local studies library in your county, but your local records office may also have copies.

Other sources of local newspapers include these.

- Online at the British Library website, though availability is limited.
- In the British Library's Newspaper Library at Colindale.

- On local library computer terminals; usually these are abstracts or full articles of more recent issues, held in intranet archives and for copyright reasons they may be available only in the main county library. These archives are often searchable if the reports are digitised, but be aware that the articles are highly likely to be within copyright.
- Online – for example the Newspaper Detectives have various nineteenth-century editions of the *Surrey Advertiser* at www.newspaper detectives.co.uk/index.htm. There may also be transcriptions from local newspapers online as part of a local history group's website or through Genuki www.genuki.org.uk.

What to expect from local newspapers

Local newspapers are particularly useful sources for:

- obituaries;
- notices of weddings;
- births and deaths;
- notable events – fires, epidemics, accidents, railways;
- criminal trials (usually reported verbatim) – general sessions and assizes, executions were usually covered as well;
- lists of people killed in wars or awarded medals;
- notices of bankruptcies;
- advertisements for local activities (e.g. events, clubs, societies) and local trades;
- sales of farms, businesses or property;
- information about licensing, e.g. if a pub received or was refused a licence – and why;
- enclosure (or 'inclosure') notices;
- information about collection of tax assessments;
- information about public buildings e.g. laying of the first stone, opening.

Potential difficulties with local newspapers

Very few local newspapers are digitised and searchable, so unless you know dates for particular events it can take a long time to comb through the archives and you might not find anything helpful. The print tends to be in a very small font, particularly for newspapers from the mid to late nineteenth century, and can be very wearing to read for long periods. Although it's possible to print copies from microfilm, it tends to be very expensive – you need to magnify the pages in order for the photocopy to be legible, so you may end up with 12 A4 sheets covering just one page of a printed newspaper.

Your local archive may not have every edition in a series of newspapers and some older newspapers may be damaged. If the original owner of the newspaper had ticked off things while reading through or circled bits of interest, some words may be illegible in the microfilm copy.

Obituaries aren't always reliable, because often the information was provided to the newspaper by family and friends – people who clearly wanted to paint a rosy picture of the deceased's life.

Be aware of political slants, too. If your local city published more than one newspaper they may be biased in favour of different parties and report things differently. For example, in Norwich there's the *Norfolk Chronicle* (a Whig paper, which tends to report events in a rather sober manner) and the *Norwich Mercury* (a Tory paper, which tends to be more colourful).

If you're intending to publish your research note the laws of copyright re quoting from a newspaper.

- For an unsigned article (i.e. the author was anonymous): copyright expires 70 years from the end of the calendar year in which the work was made, or made available to the public. So a newspaper published in 1920 was out of copyright in 1991.

◆ For a signed article (i.e. one with a byline giving the reporter's name): copyright expires 70 years from the end of the calendar year in which the author died.

Case study: using local newspapers

I had already struck lucky with the discovery of the sale notice in 1804 (see chapter 7, pages 101–2, regarding newspaper advertisements). Some of the eighteenth-century newspapers for Norfolk had been indexed by historian John Fone, so I checked to see if there were any reports for Attleborough or Attleburgh, or if any of the names mentioned in the index happened to match names on my 'occupiers and owners' list.

I found two references in the *Norfolk Chronicle and Norwich Gazette* to a Mr John Knights in Attleburgh. John Knights occupied/owned the land, according to the land tax assessments for 1800–1810, and was also listed as a baker in the town in the *Universal British Directory* 1793–8.

The first reference was on 7 April 1781 (shown here with original punctuation and spelling):

> Stolen, on Saturday Night, the 24th of last March, from Mr John KNIGHT's, Windmill, in Attleburgh, Norfolk, a black Breasted Duck-winged Cock, with white Legs, marked on one or both Norrels, three Years old, weighs upwards of five Pounds.

He was offering a reward for information, which he said should be given to Charles Hawksley, the landlord of the Cock pub in Attleborough. The Cock pub is a couple of hundred metres away from Mill House. This corroborates the evidence of Faden's map of 1797: so there was a mill in more or less the same location before the new one was built in 1804.

The second reference, from 12 April 1783 (again with original spelling and punctuation), gave me a possible clue as to what had happened to the original mill:

> John KNIGHTS, of Attleborough, in Norfolk, Miller and Baker, having assigned over his Effects to Jonathan KNIGHTS, of Carleton Rode, Miller, for the equal Benefit of his Creditors, the Creditors are requested to meet at the Cock in Attleborough, on Thursday the 24th of this Instant, April, at three o'Clock in the Afternoon, when the State of his Affairs will be laid before them, and the Assignment for the Execution. And all Persons who stand indebted to the said John KNIGHTS, are desired to pay the same forthwith to the said Jonathan KNIGHTS, or they will be sued for the same without further Notice.
> (Dated April 7, 1783.)

Was it possible that after Knights' bankruptcy the bulk of the business moved to Carleton Rode and the mill fell into disrepair?

There was another advertisement on 10 September 1796, for a 'capital post windmill, with two pair of French Stones and Going Geers [sic], in good repair' to be 'sold and removed from off the Premises'. The seller was S. N. Stephens – who built the 1804 mill on the same land, so it's possible that the old mill was either too small or too old-fashioned.

I managed to trace further changes of occupancy/ownership of the mill via the *Norfolk Chronicle*:

◆ 19 September 1807, the mill was advertised for sale again (the ad was repeated on 26 September and 3 October). The sale was to be in Norwich, in the Star inn at the Old Haymarket at 4 o'clock on 3 October. In addition to the mill, two acres of land, the dwelling-house, granaries and stable, the purchaser was offered the lease of 'eighteen acres of arable land, a baking-offices and two cottages, of which nine years will be unexpired next Michaelmas'. Potential purchasers should apply to Mr W. Harmer 'who will shew the premises'.

◆ 24 June 1809, the mill was advertised for sale again, this time offering 'a small Farm on lease' as well as the usual comments about the mill, land and buildings. This time potential purchasers should 'apply to the Printers'.

◆ 23 March 1811, the mill was up for sale again 'by order of the Assignees of Mr Robt. Bradfield, a Bankrupt'. (His bankruptcy was listed on 2 March 1811.) This time the mill and cottages were put in separate lots: lot 1 was the mill, yard, stables, and cart; lot 2 was the brick and tile dwelling house (i.e. the cottage) with baking-office, granary, cart-lodge, stable and cowhouse; lot 3 was another dwelling-house with a keeping-room, kitchen, wash-house, store-rooms, comfortable sleeping-rooms, attics, cellar, yard, garden, stables and outbuildings; lot 4 was the pasture land (the only bit that's excepted from being freehold – this would tie up with the details on the enclosure map), and lot 5 was clearly the small leased farm with 18 acres, a house and cottage, which had an 'unexpired term of six years from Michaelmas last'.

◆ 6 April 1816, Joseph Cooper (who was the occupier of the mill and house in 1815–6) had a 'Commission of Bankrupt awarded and issued forth' against him.

◆ 9 September 1826 the mill was up for sale again, together with a dwelling house, miller's cottage, barn, stables and lodges, with grassland and gardens 'well planted with choice fruit trees', and potential purchasers were directed to 'enquire of John Mann'.

◆ 28 November 1832, the mill was up for sale or to be let. John Mann, the owner, appeared to be happy to split the property into two sections: the mill with dwelling house, miller's cottage and outbuildings, and the dwelling-house and baking office adjoining it.

◆ 1 October 1836, there was another advertisement, this time for letting the mill (together with 14 acres); those interested were directed to apply to 'Mr Wm. Miles, Saddler'.

- 22 January 1842, the mill appears again – 'in full trade' together with the baking office, dwelling house, miller's cottage, barn, stable and outbuildings, and two acres of land. Those interested were directed to apply to the Post Office.
- 16 November 1861, we finally see the end of the mill: Salter and Simpson, auctioneers, were 'instructed by Mrs Wright' to sell the mill 'by auction, without reserve'. The mill had been taken down and divided into lots.

LOCAL HISTORIANS

Local historians may already have done some work on the property (perhaps as part of a larger project) and may be willing to share information with you. To find a local historian, try asking at your branch library; the staff there are quite likely to know anyone locally who's studied local records, or if there's a local history group.

The British Association for Local History www.balh.co.uk can put you in touch with local groups, or try looking up the list of groups at Local History Online www.local-history.co.uk/Groups – it's arranged by county and includes a list of national groups with specialist interests.

ORAL HISTORY

Former owners and neighbours may be able to tell you what they know of the history and may even have photographs. However, you need to bear in might that they might not want to talk to you about the house, and you might not like some of what you hear. Always be polite, and ask rather than demand.

If you're looking at a particular event that affected your house, your local radio or newspaper might run a piece and help you get in touch with people who remember the event or might have material to help you. Library staff, curators and record office staff may also be able to suggest sources.

The Oral History Society and British Sound Library Archive hold training courses around the country every year about how to interview people. The Oral History Society (www.ohs.org.uk) or your local sound archive can advise if there's a course near you.

Preparing for an interview

Once someone has agreed to talk to you about the house, you need to prepare for the interview. Make a list of questions you want to ask to get more information, but don't be too rigid about it – as the interview develops you may find more information coming out. But do keep the interview going along a loose structure, otherwise you might not get answers to the questions you wanted to ask.

When you set up the interview, your interviewee needs to know exactly what you're planning to do with the information (e.g. if giving a copy to the local sound archive, or publishing part or all of the interview in print, in broadcast or on the internet). It's a good idea to use a clearance form to make sure that everyone understands what's being planned to protect both the interviewee and interviewer.

Doing the interview

Use an audio recorder if you can. For a start, you won't be able to write as fast as your subject speaks – or be able to read your notes very easily afterwards! Using an audio recorder also helps you with eye contact and positive body language that might help encourage the person to talk to you. If you don't have your own equipment you may be able to borrow something from your local oral history group or sound archive, who can also give you more advice about preserving the recording.

A few rules of thumb:

◆ Keep questions short and clear.
◆ Use open questions (i.e. which can't be answered with yes or no).

- Don't interrupt – wait for a pause before asking the next question.
- Use positive body language – nods and smiles.
- Don't rush.
- Don't contradict or get into an argument with your subject.
- Be sensitive and respect confidences.
- Try to make smooth transitions between subjects.

Under the Data Protection Act 1998 you need to get permission before publishing the interview if your subject, or anyone else they're talking about, can be identified as individuals.

After the interview

Thank your subject for talking to you, but don't rush away. You need to give them your contact phone number and address – they may remember something later and want to tell you about it. You also need to say whether you're coming back for a further interview or not, and arrange a time if you are.

Tell them how the interview is going to be preserved (e.g. if you're going to deposit a copy in your local sound archives and keep a copy on your computer), and what you're going to do with the interview (for example: use it for research, publish or broadcast it, or transcribe it).

If your interviewee asks for any restrictions, such as no publication on the internet, you need to write these down and make sure you both sign them. You also need to discuss copyright and clearance – a form stating that you can use the recordings (a clearance form) is a very good idea. If your interviewee wants a copy of the recording or transcript, you need to make this copy and deliver it.

Copyright issues

There are separate copyrights for the words spoken and for the actual recording. The person who owns the words spoken is the speaker; the person who owns the recording is the person or organisation who arranged for it to be made. Copyright of transcriptions belongs to the owner of the words spoken.

Copyright lasts for 70 years after the end of the year in which the speaker died. If the material was recorded before 1 August 1989 copyright lasts until 50 years from the end of 1989, or 70 years after the death of the speaker, whichever is the longer.

Under the Copyright Act 1988 you also need to make sure you don't edit, adapt or alter the material to give any false impressions, regardless of who owns the copyright.

Example clearance form

[Interviewer name/project name] is grateful for your contribution of an oral history recording. As you know the recording/transcript will be preserved for posterity and used in the project.

Under the 1988 Copyright Act [I/we] need to seek your written permission to use the recording. This does not restrict any use you may wish to make of the information you gave [me/us], but it lets [me/us] ensure your contribution is preserved for posterity and used in the project and in accordance with your wishes.

[Description of items, e.g. 'John Smith's recollection of High Street, Anytown, 1953-60']

Do you have any objection to your contribution being used for:

A resource for research purposes   Yes/No
Educational use in schools, colleges etc   Yes/No

Reference and as a source of information for publications	Yes/No
Use on [the project's] website	Yes/No
Do you wish to remain anonymous?	Yes/No
Do you wish to make any time restrictions before your contribution is released?	Yes/No
Would you be willing to assign your copyright to [project/archive], which will allow [project/archive] to use your recording/transcript?	Yes/No

Signed_____
Print name_____
Address_____
Postcode_____
Telephone_____

Other issues

Oral history needs to be corroborated, as people's memories may mix up dates and names, so always check with another source if you can.

Case study: using oral history

Unfortunately, the people I would have liked to interview about the house had already passed away or, being elderly and rather frail, were too ill to be able to talk to me.

The most interesting piece of oral history about the house is something I remember from the early 1970s when I was supposedly asleep in the back of the car, and my parents started talking about the ghost of our cottage. Local lore had it that the house belonged to a miller who thought his pregnant wife had been unfaithful, murdered her in a jealous rage and threw her body down the well. He then died from septicaemia when he burned his hand on a bread oven. (It's hardly surprising that I grew up to be a romantic novelist with a taste for spooky stories!)

A local shopkeeper, a few doors further down the street, told me that the ghostly miller was well known and if she left bread in a certain room in the shop overnight it would be thrown everywhere the next morning. This might have been an adult enjoying telling a spooky story to a child, though – at the time I was too young to ask for corroboration of the evidence!

We experienced some spooky events at Mill House. I saw unexplained shadows passing the kitchen window, when I was very small; the family dogs refused to go anywhere near a certain spot in the garden and would circle it, barking, if a ball went into the area; and the dining room was always cold, even when the fire was lit. Was this to do with the mad miller and the ghost story?

Sadly, as noted in Chapter 9, I couldn't find any evidence to support the legend. The only murder in Attleborough for which I could find details was that of Martha Alden's husband Samuel in 1806 (incidentally, her ghost is meant to haunt Norwich Castle).

What's more likely is that the mill fell into mild disrepair after Knights' bankruptcy in 1783. There is a folk ballad called The Wittam Miller about the miller John Mauge from Wytham in Oxfordshire, who murdered his sweetheart Annie Kite in the eighteenth century and was hanged. This ballad is attributed to tales in several places around the country, so it's entirely possible that someone heard the ballad and thought that it probably explained why the mill became derelict, and the legend became more and more embroidered over the years. There was a case at Witton in Norfolk, where miller John Rudd Turner killed his wife Hannah and son William in 1831, was found insane and committed to the asylum; he died of natural causes in the asylum, the following year. Over the years the story could have been confused with the Attleborough mill and seen as an explanation of why the Great Mill was knocked down.

The more prosaic truth is that a new mill was built near the station, which had the advantage of better transport links and the business from the Great Mill, Dodd's Mill and the mill at Rivett's Lane simply transferred to Station Mill. The Great Mill was taken down in 1861 and according to a newspaper advertisement its various parts were auctioned off at the end of November.

Appendix 1

Common Abbreviations

Abbreviations in legal documents are usually marked by a horizontal line immediately above the abbreviated word. Obviously it's easier to read the full word than the abbreviation – but if you do decide to write the words in full when you transcribe a document, remember to put the additional letters between square brackets so you know exactly what was shown on the document and what you've interpreted.

Note that often 'ing' is abbreviated to a g (with a line just above the previous two letters of the word).

The list below refers to English abbreviations. If the document is in Latin, I would recommend Charles T. Martin's *The Record Interpreter* (see Appendix 5 on page 204 for full details).

Abbreviation	Full word or phrase	Transcribed version
Ads	administrators	ad[ministrator]s
Absly	absolutely	abs[olute]ly
Agst	against	ag[ain]st
Afrd	aforesaid	af[o]r[esai]d
Aftd	afterward	aft[erwar]d
Applon	application	appl[icati]on
Apports	apportionments	apport[ionment]s
Assis	assigns	assi[gn]s
Belongg	belonging	belong[in]g
Betn	between	bet[wee]n

Abbreviation	Full word or phrase	Transcribed version
Buildg	building	build[in]g
Comprd	comprised	compr[ise]d
condon	condition	cond[iti]on
conson	consideration	cons[iderati]on
constitg	constituting	constit[utin]g
contt	contract	cont[rac]t
coven	covenant	coven[ant]
deced	deceased	dec[eas]ed
descd	described	desc[ribe]d
disch	discharged	disch[arged]
divn	division	div[isio]n
dwghse	dwellinghouse	dw[ellin]gh[ou]se
easemts	easements	easem[en]ts
este	estate	est[at]e
exuos/exs/exors	executors	ex[ec]u[t]o[r]s or ex[ecutor]s or ex[ecut]ors
Fly (usually Fly Societies)	friendly	f[riend]ly
havg	having	hav[in]g
hrs	heirs	h[ei]rs
hereds	hereditaments	hered[itament]s
inty	indemnity	in[demni]ty
indre	indenture	ind[entu]re
insurce	insurance	insur[an]ce
mentd	mentioned	ment[ione]d
mercht	merchant	merch[an]t
mtge	mortgage	m[or]t[ga]ge
mortgees	mortgagees	mort[ga]gees
outbldgs	outbuildings	outb[ui]ld[in]gs
pt	part	p[ar]t
paymt	payment	paym[en]t
persl (usually 'persl estate')	personal	pers[ona]l
prems	premises	prem[ise]s

Abbreviation	Full word or phrase	Transcribed version
ppal	principal	p[rinci]pal
prob	probate	prob[ate]
promy	promissory	prom[issor]y
purs	purchasers	pur[chaser]s
rects	receipts	rec[eip]ts
recit	reciting	recit[ing]
redemptn	redemption	redempt[io]n
registed	registered	regist[er]ed
regy	registry	reg[istr]y
resply	respectively	resp[ective]ly
sd	said	s[ai]d
shd	should	sh[oul]d
subj	subject	subj[ect]
survor	survivor	surv[iv]or
testor	testator	test[at]or
therer	thereafter	there[afte]r
thof	thereof	th[ere]of
thrut	throughout	thr[ougho]ut
tog	together	tog[ether]
trees	trustees	tr[ust]ees
wh	which	wh[ich]
witht	without	with[ou]t
witned	witnessed	witn[ess]ed

Appendix 2

Transcription of Abstract of Title

Legal handwriting is notoriously difficult to read, so if you're transcribing a series of documents you'll find it easier to start with the latest one and work backwards to the earliest ones. Because parchment was expensive legal clerks tended to abbreviate common words (examples of which are shown in Appendix 1). It's worth persevering, however, because, the deeds can give you quite a lot of information about the people who owned or lived in the house. You may also find it's worth making yourself an 'alphabet' of the letter formations in the document – so if you come across a word you can't work out immediately, the 'alphabet' might help you work out the letters in the word or abbreviation.

The transcript below is from the deeds of Mill House, dating from 1892. In this case I've expanded the abbreviations, and any letters that aren't in the original document are shown within square brackets. Note that there is very little punctuation; this is very common in legal documents (as a look through just about any insurance policy wording from the mid 1980s will show!).

Transcription of Abstract of the title of Mr John Wright to a freehold messuage and premises in High Street Attleborough in the County of Norfolk (1892)

Lot 5 Mr Frederick Wright

RWH Venn

Attleborough

Abstract of the Title of Mr John Wright to a freehold Messuage & Premises ~~in High~~ formerly in the occupation of Martha Wright dec[eas]ed in High Street Attleborough it he County of Norfolk

1891 Oct[obe]r 13th

By Ind[entu]re so dated and made bet[wee]n Frederick Wright Yeoman and Alfred Muskell Bank Manager both of Attleboro[ugh] in the County of Norfolk of the one part & John Wright of Attleboro[ugh] af[o]r[esai]d Painter of the other part.

Reciting that of an Ind[entu]re dated the 16th May 1850 & made bet[wee]n Tho[ma]s Banks & Mary his wife of the 1st part George Bolton of the 2nd part John Wright (father of s[ai]d John Wright party th[ere]to & since dec[eas]ed) of the 3rd part & Daniel Alexander of the 4th part & duly actioned by the s[ai]d M. Banks (among other hered[itament]s) the hered[itament]s & premises desc[ribe]d in the Schedule thereto were conveyed & assured to uses in bar of dower in favour of s[ai]d J. Wright dec[eas]ed (there[afte]r called J. Wright the father) in fee simple

And recit[ing] that by an Ind[entu]re of Mort[ga]ge dated the 18th May 1850 & made bet[wee]n s[ai]d J. Wright of the one p[ar]t & Rob[er]t Joiner of the other part the s[ai]d J. Wright in cons[iderati]on of £1200 paid to him by s[ai]d R Joiner of the other part did grant (among other hered[itament]s) the hered[itament]s intended to be h[ere]by conveyed with their apport[ionment]s unto & to the use of s[aid] R. Joiner his heirs & ex[ec]u[t]o[r]s subj[ect] to a prov[iso] for redempt[io]n of s[aid] hered[itament]s on paym[en]t by s[ai]d J. Wright the father his h[eir]s &c unto s[aid] R [Joiner?] his ex[ecutor]s &c of £1200 with interest on the 18th Nov then next.

And recit[in]g s[ai]d J. Wright the father being seised in fee simple in portion subj[ect] to s[ai]d recited Ind[enture] of M[or]tg[ag]e of (inter alia) the hered[itament]s intend[e]d to be hereby conveyed duly made by his will dated 11th Oct 1856 & th[ere]by after appoint[in]g his wife Martha Wright and s[ai]d F. Wright & one James Taylor ex[ec]u[t]o[r]s thereof devised & bequeathed all his real & pers[ona]l estate unto his s[ai]d wife M. Wright and her ass[ign]s for her life she pays thereon all his [just] debts (except such as at his dec[eas]e might be due upon m[or]t[ga]ge of any p[ar]t of his real est[at]e) funeral & testancy expe[nse]s And from an in[demni]ty after her dec[eas]e s[ai]d test[at]or ordered & empowered s[ai]d F. Wright & Jas. Taylor or the surv[iv]or of them his e[xecutor]s or ad[ministrator]s at any time or times and in any manner he or they sh[oul]d think proper to sell & abs[olute]ly dispose of all his real & pers[ona]l est[ate] in one or more lot or lots either by public auction or private cont[rac]t or partly by one way & partly by the other

[p2]

with full power to enter into and sign and make any cond[iti]on or cont[rac]ts for sale they or he might think proper and to rescind or alter such cond[iti]ons or cont[rac]ts and to convey and assure the s[ai]d real est[at]e when sold unto the pur[chaser] or pur[chaser]s th[ere]of his her or their heirs or assi[gn]s or as he she or they sh[oul]d direct and to receive the proceeds of every such sale & to give rec[eip]ts for the same such rec[eip]ts to be effectual discharges & persons pay[in]g money not force to appl[icati]on th[ere]of.

And reciting that s[ai]d J. Wright the father duly made a codicil for his s[ai]d will dated 12 Oct[obe]r 1856 & th[ere]by revoked the appointm[en]t of s[ai]d Jas. Taylor as one of the Ex[ectu]ors of s[ai]d his s[ai]d will and app[oin]ted in his stead s[ai]d A. Muskell & gave to s[ai]d A. Muskell all the trusts powers author[it]ies and dir[ecti]ons wh[ich] he had in & by his s[ai]d will given to s[ai]d Jas. Taylor.

And reciting s[ai]d J. Wright the father died on 13th Oct[ober] 1856 with[ou]t hav[in]g revoked or altered his s[ai]d will & codicil wh[ich] on the 21st Feb[ruar]y following were duly proved I the Archdeaconry Court at Norwich by s[ai]d J. Wright F. Wright & A. Muskell

And reciting that by ind[entu]re dated 15th Jan[uar]y 1886 & made bet[wee]n Jas Cole Copeman W[illia]m Crickmore & John Leist Joiner of the one part and s[ai]d M. Wright of the other part s[ai]d J. C. Copeman W. Crickmore and J. L. Joiner as Ex[ecut]ors of the will & codicil duly proves & pers[ona]l repr[esentat]ives of the s[ai]d R. Joiner who died on the 6th Sept[ember] 1876 in cons[iderati]on of £1500 to them paid by s[ai]d M. Wright did assign the s[ai]d p[rinci]pal sum of £1200 secured by the thr[ougho]ut recited ind[entu]re of mortg[ag]e & certain further sums of money secured by certain prom[issor]y notes & memoranda of charge dated subsequently to s[ai]d ind[entu]re of m[or]tg[ag]e amount[in]g tog[ether] to the sum of £250 (mak[in]g tog[ether] an aggregate p[rinci]pal sum of £1550) & all m[or]t[gage] thereon to become due & all powers for securing the same unto s[ai]d M. Wright abs[olute]ly & did convey all & subj[ect] the mess[uag]es & hered[itament]s dec[eas]ed & [? conepres] in or affected by s[ai]d ind[entu]re of mortg[ag]e & in end[owe]d of charge resp[ective]ly with their appor[tionmen]ts until & to the use of s[ai]d M. Wright in fee simple subj[ect] to such right or equity of s[ai]d ind[entu]re of m[or]tg[ag]e mem[oran]da of charge & prom[issor]y notes resp[ective]ly.

And recit[in]g s[ai]d M. Wright died on the 20th March then last hav[ing] duly made her will dated the 6th March then last & th[ere]by app[oin]ted Frederick Foulsham & s[ai]d A. Muskell ex[ecut]ors &

tr[ust]ees th[ere]of who on the 21st May then last duly proved same in the P[rinci]pal Reg[istr]y of the Prob[ate] Div[isio]n of the High C[our]t of Justice

And seeing that by an in[dentu]re dated the 30th May then last & empowered

[p3]

on the last recited ind[entu]re & made bet[wee]n F. Foulsham and s[ai]d A. Muskell of the one part & s[ai]d F. Wright & s[ai]d A. Muskell of the other part and in cons[iderati]on of all principal money & with secured by the thr[ougho]ut recited ind[entu]re of the 16th Jan[uar]y 1886 hav[in]g been fr[eehol]d the s[ai]d F. Foulsham & s[ai]d A. Muskell as pers[ona]l repr[esentat]ives of s[ai]d M. Wright dec[eas]ed conveyed all the lands & prem[ise]s in the last ment[ione]d ind[entu]re unto & to the use of s[ai]d F. Wright & A. Muskell in fee simple upon the trusts ment[ione]d in the thr[ougho]ut sealed Will of s[ai]d J. Wright the father dec[eas]ed freed & disch[arged] from all p[rinci]pal & with secured by the last ment[ione]d ind[entu]re.

And recit[in]g that in excise of the prove or trust for sale cont[aine]d in the thr[ougho]ut recited will of s[ai]d J. Wright dec[eas]ed the s[ai]d F. Wright & A. Muskell put up for sale by public auction in divers lots the hered[itament]s compr[ise]d in s[ai]d Will & at wh[ich] auction the s[ai]d J. Wright party th[ere]to became the purc[haser] at the price of £890 of the properties constit[utin]g Lots 1 2 5 & 3 as the same lots were shewn on the plan thereon being the hered[itament]s compri[se]d in the schedule thereunder written subj[ect] to the prov[isi]on onto build[in]g thereon thr[ougho]ut empo[were]d & subj[ect] to the right & rights of way thr[ougho]ut referred to & (as regards Lot 5) to the duty as to fences thr[ougho]ut referred to

It was witne[sse]d that in cons[iderati]on of the sum of £890 to s[ai]d F. Wright & A. Muskell p[ai]d by s[ai[d J. Wright (p[roper]ty th[ere]to) at & the rec[eip]t & they the to s[ai]d F. Wright & A. Muskell as personal repr[esentat]ives of s[ai]d J. Wright dec[eas]ed did th[ere]by grant & convey unto s[ai]d J. Wright & his heirs.

All & every the hered[itament]s & prem[is]es 1st 2ndly 3rdly & 4thly desc[ribe]d in the schedule thereunder written & constituting resp[ective]ly as appeared from same schedule Lots 1 2 5 & 3 of s[ai]d sale and wh[ich] s[ai]d prem[is]es were shewn on the plan drawn thereon (inter alia) Lot 5 being edged yellow

Together with the right easem[en]ts and apport[ionment]s th[ere]to belong[in]g or th[ere]with enjoyed but subj[ect] as regards Lot 5 to the right & rights of way for all purposes of Lots 7 8 & 9 over the road shown by the dotted line from A to D on s[ai]d plan the s[ai]d Lots 6 7 8 & 9 on the owners th[ere]of for the time being bear[in]g and pay[ing] their due proportions for keeping the s[ai]d road & roads in repair And subj[ect] also to the restrictions onto the boundary line for buildings wh[ich] is expr[essed] in the coven[ant] of the said J. Wright thr[o]u[gho[ut] cont[inue]d.

To his the s[ai]d first 2ndly 3rdly & 4thly desc[ribe]d prem[is]es with their respective

[p4]

apport[ionment]s subject only as aft[erwar]d unto and

To the Use of the said J. Wright (party th[ere]to) in fee simple for ever

Declara[ti]on by J. Wright in bar of dower

Coven[an]t by s[ai]d J. Wright with s[ai]d & A. Muskell & also with the owners for the time being of Lots 6 7 8 10 11 12 4 & 3 that no building (other than a boundary fence) sh[oul]d be set up or built or erected on Lot 5 or on any part therefore nearer to the High St[reet] af[oremen]tione]d than was shewn by the dotted boundary or build[in]g line on the s[ai]d plan & that no build[in]g sh[oul]d be set up or built or erected on Lots 1 or 2 beyond the present frontage of the houses & shops on such two lots resp[ective]ly

Prov[is]o that the right to sue & enforce the s[ai]d restrictive coven[an]t as to b[ui]ld[in]g sh[oul]d pass to each respective pur[chase]r of Lots 3 4 5 6 7 8 10 11 & 12 & sh[oul]d be for ever thereat resp[ective]ly observed & performed by the owners for the time being of the s[ai]d lots as shewn on the s[ai]d plan & sh[oul]d be mutually enforceable by & af[??]al the s[ai]d owners for the time being resp[ective]ly & that neither s[ai]d F. Wright nor A. Muskell sh[oul]d be personally liable thereunder after the had parted with each lot resp[ective]ly.

Coven[an]t by s[ai]d J. Wright with s[ai]d F. Wright & A. Muskell that to erect & forthwith & thereat at all times to maintain & keep a substantial fence along the dottred line & to F shewn on s[ai]d plan ~~& also to keep in good repair at his own expense such part of parts of the s[aid] intended new road on the s[aid] light brown coloured land as war or were coexten-stive with the hered[itament]s & prem[is]es 1st 2ndly & 4thly thereby~~

The Schedule

Thirdly All that Messuage or Dw[ellin]gh[ou]se & paddock & pasture land fronting to the High Street af[o]r[sai]d being Lot 5 on s[ai]d plan & all outb[ui]ld[in]gs pumps yards & prem[is]es th[ere]to belong[in]g then lately in the occup[ati]on of Martha Wright dec[eas]ed but then untenanted – bounded on the north by lad of W[illia]m Miles Nicholls On the West in part by land of the Misses Francklin & on other part by the hered[itament]s forming Lots 6 7 8 & 9 on the s[ai]d plan On the south by the High Street af[ore]s[ai]d & on the east as to part by the hered[itament]s forming Lot 10 on s[ai]d plan & as to other part of the hered[itament]s thr[o]u[ghou]t 4thly ment[ion]ed.

1892 March 1st

By Ind[entu]re so dated & made bet[wee]n the s[ai]d J. Wright of the one part & W[illia]m Frederick Sparrow Painter & Decorator Charles Foulsham Licensed Victualler Theophilus John Humphrey Grocer & Draper Charles Long Merch[an]t & William Stebbings Ironmonger all of Attleboro[ugh[af[ore]s[ai]d Trustees of the Loyal

[p5]

Albemarle Lodge of the Odd Fellows F[riend]ly soc[iet]y holden at Attleboro[ugh] af[ore]s[ai]d duly regist[er]ed and numb[er]ed 3346 under the F[riend]ly Societies' Act 1875 (therein called "the Trustees") of the other part

Recit[in]g the before abstracted Ind[entu]re

And recit[in]g appor[tionmen]t for loan of £450 to s[ai]d J. Wright

It was witn[ess]ed that in cons[iderati]on of £450 to s[ai]d J. Wright on & paid by the mort[ga]gees out of the funds of the s[ai]d Soc[iet]y (the rec[eip]t &c) the s[ai]d J. Wright th[ere]by cont[ract]ed with the mort[ga]gees to pay to them £450 & int[eres]t at the rate & on the day therein ment[ione]d

And it was also witn[ess]ed that for the cons[iderati]on af[ore]s[ai]d the s[ai]d J. Wright as beneficial owner th[ere]by graunted & conveyed unto the mort[ga]gees All & every the hered[itament]s & prem[is]es 1st 2ndly & 3rdly desc[ribe]d in the Schedule th[ere]to

Tog[ether] with all the rights of every & other rights eas[e]m[en]ts & apport[ionment]s th[ere]to belong[in]g & ther[ewi]th enjoyed

To hold the same unto & To the Use of the mortg[ag]ees in fee simple subj[ect] to the prov[is]o for redempt[io]n follow[in]g viz Proviso for the redempt[io]n of s[ai]d hered[itament]s on paym[en]t by s[ai]d J. Wright his h[ei]rs & ass[ign]s accord[ing] to the foregoing coven[an]t in that behalf of £450 and ent[ere]d on the day therefore ment[ione]d

Coven[an]t by s[ai]d J. Wright for insur[an]ce of build[in]gs ag[ain]st fire & for observ[an]ce & performance of the coven[an]ts cov[enant]ed in the [?]thrub[in]gs recited ind[entu]re & to keep the mortg[ag]ees indemnified aga[ins]t any & each thereof Declar[ati]on that s[ai]d J. Wright sh[oul]d not lease with[ou]t consent ~~otherth~~ otherwise than from year to year.

The Schedule

(inter alia) The hered[itament]s & prem[is]es in the hereinbefore abstracted indenture thereby described

Appendix 3

Building a Picture of a Trade

In this case I was researching the history of a house linked to a mill. This meant that researching the millers through the trade directories would help me to build up a picture of the trade in the area – and hopefully help me pinpoint which of them lived or worked at the mill in Attleborough.

I knew from maps and other sources that there were six mills in the area.

- Haverscroft, modern-day Dodds Road – named after the long-time miller there, Thomas Dodd.
- Rivett Lane, formerly known as World's End Lane; modern-day Hargham Road – the mill is shown on Bryant's map of 1826.
- Attleburgh Great Mill, the one on the High Street – 'our' mill, which was dismantled in 1861.
- Station Mill, the station opened in 1845 and the mill there was definitely open by 1868.
- Besthorpe Tower Mill.
- Besthorpe Post Mill.

So the first step was to list the millers in the trade directories.

Directory/year	Attleborough millers listed
Universal British Directory 1793-1798	John Knights (baker) Henry Neale (miller and baker) George Turner (farmer and miller)
Holden's 1822	Thomas Dodd (miller) William Littleproud (miller) John Murrell (baker and flour dealer)

Directory/year	Attleborough millers listed
Pigot's 1830	Thomas Dodd (miller), Townmere Common Wm Harris (corn miller), Rivett Lane John Mann (miller and maltster), Attleburgh Great Mill Robert Lovett (miller), Bisthorpe [sic] Robert Palmer (miller), Bisthorpe [sic]
Robson 1839	Thomas Dodd William Harris John Mann
White's 1845	Thomas Dodd William Harris John Mann (& Shropham) Robert Lovett and & David Palmer (Besthorpe)
Hunt & Co 1850	Joshua Flowerday Robert Lovett, Besthorpe John Sayer
White 1854	Jno. Sayer Jno. Wright
Harrod's 1868	William Brittan (miller) Thomas Button (miller) Zakariah Long (maltster) Besthorpe: Robert James Lovett (miller) Richardson Baker (beer house & miller)
Post Office 1869	Thomas Button (miller) Zedekiah Long (maltster & dealer in corn, coal, malt, hops, seeds, linseed & rape cakes, offals &c) Station Sparrow & Myhill

The next step was to add in the census records 1841-61– which could help me to confirm who lived where.

Census year	Location	Name	Age	Wife's name (age)
1841	Norwich Road	Thomas Avis	80	(n/a)
	Haverscroft	William Harris	42	Harriet (40)
	Haverscroft	Thos Dodd	60	Ann (30)
	Queen Street	John Yeomans	40	Hannah (40)
	Queen Street	Elizah Yeomans	20	(n/a)
	Nr Carr Street	Robert Lovett	45	Maria (55)
	Nr Carr Street	David Palmer	35	Lydia (36)
	Besthorpe Lodge	Samuel Wright	30	(n/a)
1851	Rivett's Lane	John Sayer (master)	57	(not listed)
	Rivett's Lane	John Browne (journeyman)	24	(n/a)
	Haverscroft St	Wm Parsons	29	Anne (36)
	Mill Lane	Robert Lovett	57	Maria (67)
	Mere St	Robert Newby	40	Maria (40)
1861	Levell Street	Thomas Whitehead	31	(not listed)
	Market St	Stephen Burroughes	21	(n/a)
	Market St	Humphrey Arloum	30	(n/a)
	Mill Lane	John Lovett	31	(not listed)
	Mill Lane	Jonas Mallot	43	widowed
	Dodds Lane	Wm Parsons	40	Hannah (29)
	Mill Road	Wm Littleproud	67	Elizabeth (73)
	Mill Road	John Semmens	?	Elizabeth (58)
	Leys Lane	John Yeomans	63	Widowed
	Besthorpe	Wm Button	45	Susan (36)
	Besthorpe	Robert James Lovett	34	(not listed)

The next step was to place the people with the mills. I already knew that Attleburgh Great Mill had stopped being used before Station Mill was up and running, so I concentrated placing the millers at the Great Mill, Haverscroft, Rivett's Lane and Besthorpe, along with a section for 'unplaced' millers. I included the information I had from taxation lists, parish records, manorial records and newspaper ads.

Date	Source	High Street (Great Mill)	Haverscroft (Dodd's Road)	Rivett Lane	Besthorpe	Unplaced
1559	Will index	Robert Sparke				
1566	Will index	John Sparke				
1630	Parish register of baptisms	Thomas Howes				
1664	Hearth tax listing	Thomas Syer	n/a	n/a	n/a	n/a
1781	Newspaper advertisement	John Knights (had a cockerel stolen)	n/a	n/a	n/a	n/a
1783	Newspaper article	John Knights became bankrupt	n/a	n/a	n/a	n/a
1788	Mortimer manorial records	Existence of the mill inferred from letter to George Turner	Licence from the Lord of the Manor to George Turner to build the windmill at Haverscroft	n/a	n/a	
1793–8	Universal British Directory	John Knights, baker	George Turner	n/a	n/a	Henry Neale
1796	Newspaper ad	Old post windmill sold by S. N. Stephens				

Date	Source	High Street (Great Mill)	Haverscroft (Dodd's Road)	Rivett Lane	Besthorpe	Unplaced
1797	Faden's Map of Norfolk	Shown a bit further north (due to lettering)	Shown as being Fettle Bridge Common	Not shown	Not shown	
1804	Newspaper ad	New mill built; for sale by S. N. Stephens				
1807	Newspaper ad	Mill for sale				
1809	Newspaper ad	Mill for sale				
1811	Newspaper ad	Miller Robert Bradfield bankrupt; mill for sale				
1815	Enclosure Map	Area is 0 A 1 R 34 P Owner Jonathan Cooper	Not shown on town centre map	Not shown on town centre map	Not shown on town centre map	
1816	Newspaper ad	Miller Joseph Cooper bankrupt				
1822	Holden's Directory	John Murrell, baker and flour dealer [name is Morrell in the taxation lists]	Thomas Dodd			William Littleproud

Date	Source	High Street (Great Mill)	Haverscroft (Dodd's Road)	Rivett Lane	Besthorpe	Unplaced
1826	Bryant's Map of Norfolk	Shown on map set back from high street	Shown on map as by what we know as Dodd's Road	Shown on map just above 'Tanmoor Common'		Shown on map near Mill Lane
1826	Newspaper ad	Mill up for sale/lease by John Mann				
1830	Pigot & Co's National Commercial Directory, Norfolk & Suffolk	John Mann, miller and maltster, Attleburgh Great Mill	Thomas Dodd (miller), Townmere Common	Wm Harris (corn miller), Rivett Lane	Robert Palmer (miller), Bisthorpe [sic]	
1832	Newspaper ad	Mill up for sale/lease by John Mann				
1813–41	Parish register of baptisms	(? possibly John Yeomans)	Thomas Dodd			William Littleproud; Edward Sharman; John Rose; Robert Lock; James

Date	Source	High Street (Great Mill)	Haverscroft (Dodd's Road)	Rivett Lane	Besthorpe	Unplaced
						Ringwood; Edmund Nurse; Thomas Burroughs William Warns
1836	Newspaper ad	Mill up for lease by William Miles				
1838	Tithe Map	Building there as 'uninhabited'. Schedule: 'Cottage, Mill, Yard & Garden' owned by John Man and occupied by 'John Mann & Others'	Shown on map	Shown on map	Shown on map	Shown on map
1838	OS 1-inch map	Shown on map	Shown on map by modern Dodd's Road (to right of Workhouse Common)	Shown on map at Rivett's Lane	Shown to left of Besthorpe Hall	
1839	Robson's Directory	John Mann	Thomas Dodd	William Harris		

Date	Source	High Street (Great Mill)	Haverscroft (Dodd's Road)	Rivett Lane	Besthorpe	Unplaced
1841	Census	John Yeomans (40) at Queen Street (no number but next to the Wright family – Elizah was his son – may have worked at the Great Mill)	Thos Dodd (60) – Haverscroft district	Wm Harris (42) – Haverscroft district	Rbt Lovett (45) and Dvd Palmer (35), both nr Carr St; Saml Wright (30), Besthorpe Lodge	Thomas Avis (80) – Norwich Road
1842	Newspaper ad	Mill up for sale				
1845	White's 1845 Norfolk (directory)	John Mann (& Shropham)	Thomas Dodd	William Harris	Robert Lovett and David Palmer	
1850	Hunt's directory			John Sayer – (assume same place as 1851 census)	Robert Lovett	Joshua Flowerday
1851	Census	Wm Parsons (29) Haverscroft St		John Sayer (57), Master Miller; John Browne (24) Journeyman miller	Rbt Lovett (47); George Greengrass (apprentice) (16)	Robert Newby (Mere St, so may have been the Great Mill)

Date	Source	High Street (Great Mill)	Haverscroft (Dodd's Road)	Rivett Lane	Besthorpe	Unplaced
						Master Miller (40) – employed [number illegible, possibly 8] men
1854	White's directory	Jno. Wright [we know cottage is owned by John Wright by then]		Jno. Sayer (assume not moved from 1851)	Robert Lovett, Besthorpe	
1861	Newspaper ad	Mill dismantled and parts for sale by Mrs Wright				
1861	Census		Wm Parsons (40)		Robert James Lovett (34); John Lovett (31); Jonas Mallot (43); Wm Button (45)	Stephen Burroughes (aged 21, lived at Market Street); Humphrey Arloum (aged 30, lived at Market Street);

Date	Source	High Street (Great Mill)	Haverscroft (Dodd's Road)	Rivett Lane	Besthorpe	Unplaced
						Wm Littleproud (aged 67, lived at Mill Road); John Semmens (lived at Mill Road); John Yeomans (aged 63, lived at Leys Lane); Thomas Whitehead (aged 31; lived at Levell Street)
1868	Harrod's directory				Robert James Lovett; Richardson Baker	William Brittan; Thomas Button
1869	Post Office directory					Thomas Button

Date	Source	High Street (Great Mill)	Haverscroft (Dodd's Road)	Rivett Lane	Besthorpe	Unplaced
1875	Post Office directory				Geo Greenacre	Frederick Charles Hart; William Beales
1877	Harrod's directory					William Beales
1881	Census				George Greenacre (45)	
1883	White's Directory			William Ketteringham	Geo Greenacre	
1884	OS Map	Mill no longer shown	Shown on map as 'disused'		Besthorpe mills shown	
1890	White's Directory			Arthur Andrews; William Ketteringham	George Greenacre	
1892	Kelly's Directory				George Greenacre	Herbert Chas Betts (wind and steam miller)
1896	Kelly's Directory		Arthur Cook & Son (millers, wind & steam) New Mill			

Appendix 4

Building a Picture of Occupants/Owners

Once I'd been through the deeds, manorial records, census returns, maps, taxation records and street directories, I was able to put together the information to build up a picture of who owned the property or lived there. There are still gaps because there are gaps in the taxation records and the owners named in the earliest set of deeds didn't marry, have children or die in the parish because they're not named in the parish records.

Date	Source	Information
Mar 1969 to 2000	Deeds	Owner G. Brighton/J. R. Sewell; occupier the Sewell family
5 Aug 1960 to Mar 1969	Deeds	Owner G. Brighton; various occupants including RAF personnel on temporary rental contracts
10 Feb 1960 to 5 Aug 1960	Deeds	Owner F. Allum
26 Mar 1953 to 10 Feb 1960	Deeds	Owner F. Allum/G. Page (?)
6 Jan 1953 to 26 Mar 1953	Deeds	Owner F. Allum
12 Oct or 29 Nov 1921 to 6 Jan 1953	Deeds	Owner R. B. Hardy
1931–1947	Rate books	Owner Charles Howard; occupier William Stone
18 Oct 1912 to 12 Oct 1921	Deeds	Owner Charles Henry Howard

Date	Source	Information
1914-1925	Rate books	Occupier Gathergood family; 1914 William M. Gathergood; 1925 E. Gathergood
10 Nov 1897 to 18 Oct 1912	Deeds	Owner Frederick/Anna Wright; tenant (1912) is William Mitchell Gathergood
1901	Census	Listed as '23' Connaught Plain, occupier Anna Wright, widow
15 March 1893	Deeds	Owner Frederick Wright/Anna Wright
10 Nov 1892	Deeds	Owner F. Wright, bought from J. Wright – property described as 'formerly in the occupation of Martha Wright deceased and late of Joseph Mann'
13 Oct 1891	Deeds	Owner J. Wright – abstract of title describes 'freehold messuage and premises formerly in the occupation of Martha Wright deceased in High Street Attleborough'
23 June 1891	Sale particulars	Auction of the estates of 'the late Mr John Wright and Mrs Martha Wright, deceased'
1891	Census	Occupier Emma Thompson (with her aunts Alice and Amelia Wright)
15 Jan 1886	Indenture (deeds)	M. Wright paid the mortgage and had rights to the house 'absolutely'
1883	White's Directory	Mrs Martha Wright noted as 'private resident'
1881	Census	'32' Mill Yard, Levell Street: occupier is Martha Wright, widow, age 70, 'cottage owner'
1875	Post Office directory	Mrs Wright noted as 'private resident'
1871	Census	'33' Mill Yard, Market Street: occupier is Martha Wright, widow, aged 60

Date	Source	Information
1861	Advertisement in *Norwich Gazette and Norfolk Chronicle*	Mill taken down in November and for sale in various lots
1861	Census	'34' Mill Yard, Market Street: occupier is Martha Wright, widow, age 50
11 Oct 1856	Deeds	John Wright bequeathed house to his wife Martha Wright
May 1850	Deeds	Thomas Banks & Mary his wife sold to John Wright (snr)
1845	Tithe map and apportionment	Owner: William Stannard Cockell; occupied by 'John Mann & Others'; property described as cottages, Mill Yard and Garden, arable land with an area of 5 roods and 21 perches
1845	White's Directory of Norfolk	Miller: John Mann
1842	Advertisement in *Norwich Gazette and Norfolk Chronicle*	Mill again for sale or to let
1841	Census	(possibly as 'Queen Street'): occupier (possibly) miller John Yeomans
1839	Robson's Directory	John Mann
1836	Advertisement in *Norwich Gazette and Norfolk Chronicle*	William Miles, Saddler, offered the lease of the mill
1832	Land Tax Assessments	Landlord John Mann; occupier James Mann

Date	Source	Information
1832	Advertisement in *Norwich Gazette and Norfolk Chronicle*	Owner John Mann put the property up for sale or lease
1830	Pigot's Directory	John Mann, (miller and maltster), Attleburgh Great Mill
1828–31	Land Tax Assessments	Landlord John Mann; occupier James Mann
1827	Land Tax Assessments	Landlord John Mann; occupier David Moore
1826	Land Tax Assessments	Landlord John Mann; occupier John Morrell
1826	Advertisement in *Norwich Gazette and Norfolk Chronicle*	Owner John Mann put the property up for sale or lease
1823	Land Tax Assessments	Landlord John Mann; occupier Wm Margason
1817–18	Land Tax Assessments	Landlord John Cooper; occupier Charles Mary
1816	Announcement in *Norwich Gazette and Norfolk Chronicle*	Miller Joseph Cooper declared bankrupt
1814	Poor rate assessments	Reference to Joseph Cooper
1813–16	Land Tax Assessments	Landlord John Cooper; occupier Thomas Cooper
1811–12	Land Tax Assessments	Landlord John Cooper; occupier John Cooper

Date	Source	Information
1811	Advertisement in *Norwich Gazette and Norfolk Chronicle*	Owner/occupier Robert Bradfield declared bankrupt and the mill and house sold
1810	Land Tax Assessments	(Possibly landlord) John Knights; occupier Mr Brown
1804–9	Land Tax Assessments	Landlord John Knights; occupier J. Knights & others
1809	Advertisement in *Norwich Gazette and Norfolk Chronicle*	'Capital Tower Windmill, nearly new' for sale; apply to the printers [of the newspaper] for particulars
1807	Advertisement in *Norwich Gazette and Norfolk Chronicle*	'Capital Tower Windmill, nearly new' for sale; apply to W. Harmer for particulars
1804	Advertisement in *Norwich Gazette and Norfolk Chronicle*	Brand new mill and cottage; seller Stephen Nobbs Stevens, millwright Nathaniel Lock
1800–1803	Land Tax Assessments	Landlord John Knights; occupier himself
1796	Advertisement in *Norwich Gazette and Norfolk Chronicle*	Old post windmill being sold by S. N. Stephens
1793–8	Universal British Directory	John Knights, baker

Date	Source	Information
1783	Announcement in *Norwich Gazette and Norfolk Chronicle*	John Knights became bankrupt and handed his business to Jonathan Knights
1781	Advertisement in *Norwich Gazette and Norfolk Chronicle*	John Knights (had a cockerel stolen)
1664	Hearth tax listing	Thomas Syer
1659	Manorial rental	Reference to a highway leading from the windmill
1638	Manorial rental	Reference to 'Myll Field' – tenant Robert ?Slomer
1630	Parish register (burials)	Thomas Howes
1623	Manorial rental	Reference to mill field, cottage and yard (tenant not named)
1566	Will index	John Sparke; bequeathed the mill to his son Valentyne.
1559	Will index	Robert Sparke; bequeathed the mill to his wife Elizabeth until his son Richard was age 21

Appendix 5

Useful Reference Books

ARCHITECTURE/HOUSE HISTORY

Nick Barratt, *Tracing the History of Your House*, The National Archives 2006, ISBN 1903365902

Bill Breckon and Jeffrey Parker, *Tracing the History of Houses*, Countryside Books reprinted 1994, ISBN 185306128X

R.W. Brunskill, *Vernacular Architecture: an Illustrated Handbook*, Faber, fourth edition 2000, ISBN 0571195032

Pamela Cunnington, *How Old is Your House?*, Marston House, 2nd edition 1999, ISBN 1899296085

Mac Dowdy, Judith Miller and David Austin, *Be Your Own House Detective*, BBC Books 1997, ISBN 0563383143

David Iredale and John Barrett, *Discovering Your Old House*, fourth edition, Shire Publications 2002, ISBN 0747804982

Nikolaus Pevsner, *The Buildings of England* series, Penguin (various dates)

Anthony Quiney, *The Traditional Buildings of England*, Thames and Hudson 1995, ISBN 0500276617

MAPS AND DOCUMENTS

Geraldine Beech and Rose Mitchell, *Maps for Family and Local History*, The National Archives 2004, ISBN 1900365503

L. C. Hector, *The Handwriting of English Documents*, Kohler & Coombes Ltd 1980, ISBN 0903967162

Charles T. Martin, *The Record Interpreter*, Phillimore, reprinted 1999, ISBN 0850334659

Lionel Munby, Steve Hobbs and Alan Crosby, *Reading Tudor and Stuart handwriting*, British Association for Local History, second edition 2002, ISBN 1860772374

Philip Riden, *Record Sources for Local History*, B.T. Batsford Ltd 1987, ISBN 0713457260

Denis Stuart, *Manorial Records: an introduction to their transcription and translation*, Phillimore 1992, ISBN 0850338212

Denis Stuart, *Latin for Local and Family Historians*, Phillimore 1995, ISBN 0850339847

GENEALOGY

Mark D. Herber, *Ancestral Trails: The Complete Guide to British Genealogy and Family History*, Sutton Publishing 2005, ISBN 0750941987

GENERAL

Joy Bristow, *The Local Historian's Glossary of Words and Terms*, Countryside Books 2001, ISBN 1853067075

C. R. Cheney (revised by Michael Jones), *A Handbook of Dates for Students of British History*, Cambridge University Press reprinted 2004, ISBN 0521770955

David Hey, *The Oxford Companion to Local and Family History*, Oxford University Press 2002, ISBN 0198606672

Lionel Munby, *How Much Is That Worth?*, Phillimore 1989, ISBN 0850337410

Colin Waters, *A Dictionary of Old Trades, Titles and Occupations*, Countryside Books 2002, ISBN 1853067946

Appendix 6

Useful Websites

GENERAL ARCHIVES INFORMATION

National Archives

www.nationalarchives.gov.uk/default.htm

Includes the Historic Manuscripts Commission and former Public Record Office. Has a detailed list of archive repositories, from local record offices and libraries through to museums and specialist archives, at www.nationalarchives.gov.uk/archon. Also has a searchable catalogue of the collections within the National Archives at http://www.nationalarchives.gov.uk/catalogue/search.asp. Extensive and very useful information leaflets and research guides.

Scottish General Register Office

www.scotlandspeople.gov

Information about Scots archival holdings.

Access to Archives (A2A)

www.a2a.org.uk

English strand of the UK Archives Network. You can search detailed catalogues from over 340 repositories (including the National Archives).

British Library

www.bl.uk

British Library website. The catalogue listings are at www.bl.uk/catalogues/listings.

Guildhall library

www.cityoflondon.gov.uk/Corporation/leisure_heritage/libraries_archives_
museums_galleries/city_london_libraries/guildhall_lib.htm

Website for the Guildhall library. Has catalogue listings plus some useful leaflets on getting started in research.

Archives hub

www.archiveshub.ac.uk

Good gateway to archives – searchable.

GENERAL HISTORICAL SOURCES INCLUDING ASSOCIATIONS

British History Online

www.british-history.ac.uk

A joint site from the Institute of Historical Research and the History of Parliament Trust; has digital resources, which you can search by county. You can also browse some Series One Ordnance Survey maps on the site.

British Association of Local History

www.balh.co.uk

Publishes a quarterly journal, *The Local Historian*, and a quarterly magazine, *Local History News*; site has membership details and good links to national organisations and local societies.

History.uk.com

www.history.uk.com

Site contains a variety of historical links. There are editorial features and a timeline.

Institute of Historical Research

www.history.ac.uk

Resources for historians including articles and an open access library.

Local History **magazine**

www.local-history.co.uk

Website has information leaflets and good links to local history societies and courses.

Royal Historical Society Bibliography

www.rhs.ac.uk/bibl/bibwel.asp

Searchable bibliographical guide to what has been written about British and Irish history from the Roman period to the present day. Hosted by the Institute of Historical Research. Includes links to online catalogues.

SOURCES FOR PEOPLE, CENSUS RECORDS AND FAMILY HISTORY

Church of Jesus Christ of Latter Day Saints (aka Family History Centres)

www.familysearch.org

Holds searchable versions of the International Genealogical Index and the 1881 census of England and Wales.

1837online.com

www.1837online.com

Access to the registers of births, deaths and marriages in England and Wales from 1837 to the present day (on a pay-per-view basis). Also has articles and advice on getting started.

Rootsweb

freebmd.rootsweb.com

Free searchable access to the index of births, deaths and marriages in the UK.

Ancestry.co.uk

www.ancestry.co.uk

Access to the 1871, 1891 and 1901 censuses of England and Wales, plus other records from the 1500s onwards. Subscription site; some free (limited) databases. You will need to register.

1901censusoline.com

www.1901censusonline.com

It's free to search the indexes although you'll pay a small fee to see the census pages and transcripts.

Society of Friends (Quakers)

www.quaker.org.uk

Information about the Society of Friends and their record holdings in the library. Can seach online, but if you want to go in person you need a dated letter of recommendation from 'someone of good standing in your community' – such as a letter from your minister if you are a member of another church; or from your tutor or supervisor if you are a student.

Federation of Family History Societies

www.ffhs.org.uk

Website has a directory of family history societies across the country.

Familia

www.familia.org.uk

Directory of family history resources held in public libraries.

Genuki

www.genuki.org.uk

Virtual reference library of information relevant to the UK and Ireland. Has good information about how to get started.

Society of Genealogists

www.sog.org.uk

Information about the Society of Genealogists and their record holdings in the library (which you can search for a fee). Also has a range of information leaflets.

Documents Online

www.documentsonline.pro.gov.uk

Searchable indexes from the 1300s to 1858.

Cyndi's List

www.cyndislist.com

Excellent genealogical resource; has some good tips for beginners at www.cyndislist.com/beginner.htm

Oxford Dictionary of National Biography (ODNB)

www.oxforddnb.com

SOURCES FOR BUILDINGS AND ARCHITECTURE

English Heritage

www.english-heritage.org.uk

Free site with details of listed buildings and the English Monuments Record.

Looking at Buildings

www.lookingatbuildings.org.uk

Joint site between the Pevsner Architectural Guides and the Buildings Books Trust. Gives information about building types, styles and materials, methods of construction, glossary, list of architects and discusses buildings in some English cities.

Pastscape

www.pastscape.org/homepage

Searchable database of listed buildings and information about finds in the areas.

Bricks and Brass

www.bricksandbrass.co.uk

Site with architectural details for nineteenth and twentieth century houses.

Land Registry

www.landregisteronline.gov.uk

Site for the Land Registry; from here you can obtain a copy of the title register details and title plan for your property (in England and Wales) for a small fee.

SOURCES FOR STREET DIRECTORIES
Historical Directories

www.historicaldirectories.org

Project from the University of Leicester that gives a searchable digital library of local and trade directories for England and Wales 1750-1919. Runs of directories are not complete, but there are several directories for most areas.

SOURCES FOR IMAGES
Heritage Image Partnership

www.heritage-images.com

Searchable library of images which you can view in thumbnail.

Images of England

www.imagesofengland.org.uk

Part of the English Heritage website. Digital library of photographs of England's 370,000 listed buildings. Has optional registration (free) for advanced search facilities.

SOURCES FOR NEWSPAPERS
***The Times* digital archive**

www.galegroup.com/Times

Searchable resource for issues of *The Times* 1785-1985. Subscription may be accessible through your local library.

SOURCES FOR TRIALS
Old Bailey proceedings

www.OldBaileyOnline.org

Proceedings of the Central Criminal Court in London from April 1674 to October 1834 – contains 101,102 trials which are digitised and fully searchable.

Newgate Calendar

www.exclassics.com/newgate/ngintro.htm

Online copy of the Newgate Calendar – trials up until the nineteenth century.

SOURCES FOR MAPS

Ordnance Survey maps

www.ordsvy.gov.uk

Digital Historical Maps

www.old-maps.co.uk

Searchable by place name, address or co-ordinate (Ordnance Survey Grid reference).

MISCELLANEOUS

Oral History Society

www.ohs.org.uk

Good practical tips on working with oral history.

Pub History Society

www.pubhistorysociety.co.uk

Current Value of Old Money

www.ex.ac.uk/%7ERDavies/arian/current/howmuch.html

Excellent resource for links on purchasing power.

English Handwriting 1500-1700

www.english.cam.ac.uk/ceres/ehoc

Online palaeography tutorial from Cambridge University – really good!

Palaeography tutorial – National Archives

www.nationalarchives.gov.uk/palaeography

Excellent tutorial.

Vision of Britain

www.visionofbritain.org.uk/index.jsp

A vision of Britain between 1801 and 2001. Including maps, statistical trends and historical descriptions written on journeys around Britain between the twelfth and nineteenth centuries. Using census information, the site demonstrates changes across Britain through the use of maps and graphs. Produced by the Department of Geography at the University of Portsmouth.

Mills Archive

www.millsarchive.com

Resource for properties that were formerly watermills or windmills.

Parish Register Transcription Society

www.prtsoc.org.uk

Information about transcriptions of parish registers.

Index

How To Research Local History

PAMELA BROOKS

This book will help get you started in research: how to interpret documents such as census returns, rating books and maps, and where to find them. It will introduce you to the delights of street directories and old newspapers, as well as leading you to websites that can save you a lot of research time and taking you through how to research in archives.

ISBN 978-1-84528-129-2

@ home with your Ancestors.com

How to research family history using the internet

DIANE MARELLI

If you'd like to be able to discover at least five generations of your family history all you need is *this book* and access to the Internet. Following on from her previous book, *Meet Your Ancestors* Diana Marelli provides you with the knowledge you need to build the history of your ancestors without leaving the comfort of your own home. Using only the Internet, you will be able to source Birth, Marriage and Death Registers (BMD); locate, access and print Census information from 1841; locate and print Parish Records; build your family tree through a combination of these and other resources and set up a family history database to record and store your findings.

By the end of this book you will become proficient at genealogical research. And you will be able to provide your children and future generations with a picture of how their families evolved over at least five generations.

ISBN 978-1-84528-177-9

Tracing Your Roots

An inspirational and encouraging introduction to discovering your family's past

DIANE MARELLI

'The best easy-to-read guide you will come across should you be considering researching your own family's history.' *Surrey Advertiser*

'This four-year diary charts one genealogist's quest to trace her ancestry. With tips on using the internet, church records, and public archives, this will prove an enormous help.' *Good Book Guide*

'Quite unlike the standard guidebook which sometimes reads like a text book, this diary engages the reader and, by way of example, passes on valuable hints and tips for anyone starting out on the genealogy trail.' *Practical Family History*

'Diane Marelli explains the whole process in straightforward and humorous language.' www.largsnews.com/libraries

'Everything is contained within this book: the highs, the lows, the joys and the sadness as dead ends are reached and more facts uncovered. Diane Marelli's quest consumed her life for four years and the final result is a joy to read and an encouragement for us all.' *Family Tree*

'A very interesting and enjoyable new approach to family history.' *Family History Monthly*

'A must in the search for your own roots.' *The Good Book Guide*

ISBN 978-1-84528-185-4

Writing Your Life Story

How to record and present your memories for friends and family to enjoy

MICHAEL OKE

'Offers hundreds of ideas, memory joggers and techniques that will help the novice bring their story to life.' – *Goodtimes Magazine*

'It's often said that everyone has a book in them. A book offering tips on writing an autobiography was heard on Steve Wright's show. This was Michael Oke's *Writing Your Life Story*.' – *Books in the Media*

'Making a professional job of your autobiography is a very worthwhile project and *Writing Your Life Story* will help you make a polished job of it.' – *Writing Magazine*

ISBN 978-1-84528-133-5

Times of Our Lives

The essential companion for writing your own life story

MICHAEL OKE

'Surprise yourself as you unlock hundreds of memories of yesteryear. Whether you are looking to write your life story, or simply enjoy reminiscing, you will be amazed at what you remember with the help of this book.' – *Daily Telegraph*

ISBN 978-1-85703-970-2

Tracking Down Your Ancestors

DR HARRY ALDER

'The book offers some expert observations on "tearless transcrib-ing" or making notes from original documents for future reference... Dr Alder uses his professional expertise to advise researchers on achieving success in bringing family history to life.' – *Practical Family History*

ISBN 978-1-85703-828-6

How To Publish Your Own Book

Everything you need to know about the self-publishing process

ANNA CROSBIE

'If you know nothing about book publishing this guide will give many of the answers. It is well researched and the author has not limited it to her own experience. She has also included a section on how to sell your book.' – *Writers Forum*

'If you read this book before you embark on a self-publishing project you will approach the job with much more confidence.' – *Writing Magazine*

ISBN 978-1-84528-106-9

Touch Type in Ten Hours

Spend a few hours now and gain a valuable skill for life

ANN DOBSON

Now in a revised and expanded 2nd edition to include the basics of Word - so you can move from touch typing to mail merge in no time at all!

With Ann Dobson's method you really can learn to touch type in ten hours – in the comfort of your own home and at the cost of this book. The easy to use lessons are divided into manageable, one hour blocks and there are plenty of exercises to consolidate what you have learned.

ISBN 978-1-84528-169-4

Learning to Read Music

Make sense of those mysterious symbols and bring music alive

PETER NICKOL

'A lucid account of the rudiments of sight-reading and music theory.' – *BBC Music Magazine*

'...useful for non-specialist primary teachers, who often find teaching music a daunting business.' – *Music Journal*

'Learning to read music can be very daunting. This compact but useful book proved excellent. It is good for reinforcing what has been learnt and excellent to keep alongside your favourite pieces of music.' – *Education Otherwise*

ISBN 978-1-84528-084-0

How To Books are available through all good bookshops, or you can order direct from us through Grantham Book Services.

Tel: +44 (0)1476 541080
Fax: +44 (0)1476 541061
Email: orders@gbs.tbs-ltd.co.uk

Or via our website
www.howtobooks.co.uk

To order via any of these methods please quote the title(s) of the book(s) and your credit card number together with its expiry date.

For further information about our books and catalogue, please contact:

How To Books
Spring Hill House
Spring Hill Road
Begbroke
Oxford
OX5 1RX

Visit our web site at
www.howtobooks.co.uk

Or you can contact us by email at info@howtobooks.co.uk